W9-BML-110

# MYSTICISM
## ITS MEANING & MESSAGE

GEORGIA HARKNESS

ABINGDON PRESS
Nashville New York

*Library of Congress Cataloging in Publication Data*

HARKNESS, GEORGIA ELMA, 1891–Mysticism: its meaning and message. Includes bibliographical references.
1. Mysticism. I. Title.
BV5082.2.H37 248′.22 72-10070

*ISBN 0-687-27667-5*



MANUFACTURED BY THE PARTHENON PRESS AT
NASHVILLE, TENNESSEE, UNITED STATES OF AMERICA

# Acknowledgments

I wish, as always, to express my gratitude to Verna Miller, the friend with whom I have shared a home for nearly thirty years, whose love and encouragement sustains me in my writing and still more in the many aspects of our life together.

Warm thanks are also due to my friend and former pastor, Pierce Johnson, who has read the manuscript in full with many helpful suggestions. His familiarity with the history and literature of this field continues to amaze me. His recent book, *Dying into Life: A Study in Christian Life Styles,* has been of special help in the sections on John of the Cross and Dag Hammarskjöld.

And, as always, I am grateful to the editors of the Abingdon Press, who with much patience and helpfulness continue to publish my books year after year.

# Preface

The theme which is designated by the title of this book has had wide fluctuations in popular interest. A few years ago—perhaps even as recently as a decade ago—mysticism was being dismissed as something archaic, occult, self-centered, pious, and contrary to any true understanding of the Christian life. What mattered was social action and a rationally grounded theology geared to the demands of the current scene. These are, indeed, legitimate and vital interests which this author believes in deeply and has no wish to disparage. Yet they are not all there is of Christian living, nor even of the most deeply grounded humanism. Said Pascal, "The heart has its reasons, which the reason cannot know." This truth continues to prove itself in experience, and one result of it is an upsurge of interest in mysticism.

Yet it must be made clear at the outset that much which is called mysticism today is a long way from it. Mysticism is not astrology, fortune-telling, clairvoyance, or spiritualism in any of the forms usually connoted by this term. It is not mental telepathy or anything which commonly goes by the name of extrasensory perception. It is not visions, auditions, locutions, or raptures. In short, it is not something superstitious or supernatural in the sense of the occult. There is mystery about it, as in all the deep things of the human spirit, but this does not mean that it can be equated with anything "misty." It is unfortunate that the term carries so many of these connotations, but it is too late to change it now.

In chapter one I shall attempt to say at some length what mysticism is. For the present, it is enough to say that it centers in the presence of God within the human spirit. Thus it is religion at its deepest and most inward level. One of my vivid memories from college days was hearing an eminent preacher of that period, Dr. Lyman Abbott, say in the university chapel, "Religion is the life of God in the soul of man." This I still believe, and it is on this profound yet simple truth that mysticism rests.

The reader will soon discover that I do not define mysticism in as exclusive terms as is sometimes done; that is, as being solely the way of negation by which all self-consciousness is stripped away until the individual feels that he is in complete identity with God. This is one kind of mysticism, but it is not the only kind. There is another understanding of it which accents "the practice of the presence of God" in daily life, and this is the key to a large amount of the Christian devotional writing of the centuries. Thus in considering the message of mysticism to the world of today I shall not hesitate to include this type, or to give attention to what may even be called "piety" if one does not use this term in too disparaging a sense.

The book falls into two main divisions. In part one I shall attempt to present the theoretical groundwork of the study. I shall try to say what mysticism is and by what criteria its forms are to be distinguished, both from each other and from religion as a whole. Then we shall trace the biblical roots of Christian mysticism. This will call for an examination of the reasons why the Old Testament, for the most part, moves along other than mystical lines. Since the main sources of Christian mysticism are to be found in the Gospel of John and in the Christ-mysticism which pervades Paul's letters, these must be examined. Yet Christian mysticism, like every other kind, has its philosophical assumptions. Furthermore, it has early philosophical rootage which considerably influenced the course of the subsequent Western tradition. After an examination of these and of the moot question of the objective reality of the mystic's experiences, the book moves to a different type of study.

Mysticism is a perennial and worldwide phenomenon. Some attempt is made in part one to place Christian mysticism in relation to this wider setting. But so extensive is the scope of mystical experience and so varied are its forms that I should be unable, even if I had the expertise, to cover all the types of Oriental mysticism along with the Christian without doing injustice to the latter. I must be content, therefore, to refer the reader to a number of excellent general surveys and center attention mainly on the Christian stream. In this area I feel a fair degree of assurance, having taught a course in "Mysticism and the Devotional Classics" for some twenty years at Garrett Theological Seminary and the Pacific School of Religion.

With the more theoretical groundwork laid in part one, part two consists of interpretative presentations of some of the great

Christian devotional and mystical writings. No anthology is included, but I shall try to include citations of enough choice and meaningful passages to give the flavor of the works and to suggest some of their permanent values. The devotional life, unlike theology, is relatively timeless and independent of its historical setting. Yet never wholly, and I shall attempt to say enough about each author and his times to make clear what underlies and gives direction to the writing.

Not all of the Christian devotional classics or their authors can be included. To do so would run the book far out of bounds as to size and hence cost. Selections will be made from a blend of three criteria: the permanent importance of the writing as a living contribution, its distinctiveness as a type, and its need of clarification in order to be read fruitfully. Any writing which does not qualify under one and preferably two of these criteria has regretfully been omitted.

But what of contemporary mysticism? Some twentieth-century mystics will be included in the series, with the prognosis that their works will live. But the kind of mysticism most in vogue today, whether Christian, Islamic, Hindu, or Zen Buddhist, whether drug-induced as part of a hippie trip or more soberly secular, is something quite different from classical mysticism. Yet it should not be bypassed as if it did not exist. Insofar as it is mysticism—and to sort out its varied strands to determine how much of it qualifies is no simple process—it needs to be given respectful attention. This I shall try to do in the last chapter. The reader who is interested only in this contemporary kind of mysticism may go at once to this chapter, if he desires, and omit all the rest. But I shall be much disappointed if he does, for the Now generation has much to learn from the past.

In short, the primary aim of the book is to present some bases for a better understanding of the mysticism of the ages, and especially that which is found in the Christian devotional classics. In part two I hope to introduce the reader afresh to a number of great figures from the past, whose names may be well known but whose inner springs of action may not be. Furthermore, I am enough of an evangelist to hope that from the book as a whole, and especially from the citations included from these writers, some readers may themselves be quickened by the power of God to a deeper devotional life.

# Contents

# PART ONE

# I

# Definitions and Distinctions

Why another book on mysticism at this time? Is not this a subject of concern only to the saints of old and the avant-garde younger generation of today, both these groups being at cross purposes with the mainstream of contemporary life? Indeed, is not mysticism a somewhat abnormal human phenomenon, with its devotees inevitably a bit "queer"? So many suppose, and we must see.

Meanwhile, our times appear to be considerably out of joint. There is no need to use many words to describe the contemporary scene, but most would agree that its dominant mood is one of pessimism, distrust of the future, lack of confidence in the meaningfulness of existence. Along with these attitudes there has been not only rapid social change in external conditions but a large-scale shift in moral standards, for better or for worse. The dominant feature of our time is paradox—amazing technological power and with it a dismal sense of personal frustration among millions, comforts and luxuries formerly undreamed of and with them a persisting malaise, greatly expanded educational opportunities without a corresponding increase in wisdom, leisure without creativity or satisfaction in the enjoyment of it. In short, there is something seriously lacking in the zest for life.

The relation of all this to mysticism and to the inner life? The relation of the second of these terms to the situation around us and in us is perhaps more obvious than is the first. Society is made up of persons, and what transpires in the interior of persons must inevitably both reflect and affect the external situation. Almost fifty years ago, in 1923, A. E. Wiggam wrote in *The New Decalogue of Science*, a book much read and quoted in that day, "If hope and courage go out of the lives of common men it is all up with social and political civilization." [1] These words were uttered at a time when hope and courage were on have inadequately fed. There is a turning, especially among the young, toward the gospel songs of an earlier day, with their rhythm and emotional appeal. "Amazing Grace" has become a popular recording, and the youth choir of the church where I worship recently rendered it with great dignity and reverence. Folk celebrations have become common in the churches, some of them raucous, some of them more novel and entertaining than worshipful, but others reflecting meaningfully the joy in the Lord to which as Christians we are all enjoined. The drug-induced "trip," appallingly common and dangerous, is not religious mysticism in an authentic sense; yet it must be mentioned because it is sought when deep inner needs are not more creatively and safely met. It is significant that one of the commonest forms of witness given by the young "Jesus people" of the streets and the "children of God" communes, and likewise of the followers of Meher Baba and Maharishi Mahesh Yogi, is that their new-found religion has enabled them to break the drug habit. In recent years glossolalia, or the speaking in tongues, which is tangent to mysticism and perhaps a form of it, has spread beyond the Pentecostal and into the mainline churches.

## 1. What Is Mysticism?

Mysticism is not an easy word to define. However, we must attempt to clarify its meaning before going further. Not all of the prejudice against the term is due to false assumptions as to its meaning, but much of it is.

Perhaps the best way to begin is to say what mysticism is not. In the German language there are two words for what in English we must designate with one. *Mystizismus* is used for the abnormal phenomena or occult pseudo-knowledge often disparaged in scientific inquiries, and *mystik* for true mysticism. The latter centers in the belief that the human spirit, finite, limited, and clouded though it is, can nevertheless experience the presence of the Divine Reality which undergirds and permeates the world. This conviction, though central, is easily distorted into weird forms of the supernatural, and thus into ideas and practices which may have popular appeal but little substance. It is characteristic of our time that more than a few of them are now in vogue in spite of our supposedly advanced scientific and cultural climate.

I have found no better list of these aberrations, or one more applicable to the American present, than is found in *Western Mysticism* by Dom Cuthbert Butler, a classic treatment of its theme which was published in England in 1922. He writes:

> There is probably no more misused word in these our days than "mysticism." It has come to be applied to many things of many kinds: to theosophy and Christian science; to spiritualism and clairvoyance; to demonology and witchcraft; to occultism and magic; to weird psychical experiences, if only they have some religious colour; to revelations and visions; to other-worldliness, or even mere dreaminess and impracticality in the affairs of life; to poetry and painting and music of which the motif is unobvious and vague. It has been identified with the attitude of the religious mind that cares not for dogma or doctrine, for church or sacraments. . . . And, on the other side, the meaning of the term has been watered down: it has been said that the love of God is mysticism; or that mysticism is only the Christian life lived on a high level; or that it is Roman Catholic piety in extreme form.[3]

Add astrology and the alleged determining of destiny by the signs of the zodiac, and we have a fairly clear picture of what passes as mysticism today, though passing by at a considerable distance from its real nature.

Doubtless some of these misconceptions arise from the fact that the word mysticism so easily suggests mystery—a mystery that has to do with more than the natural order of time and space. From this it is a short step to the conclusion that the "supernatural" means the "occult." That there is mystery in the relation of the human to the divine at any level need not be denied. But this does not mean that the essential element in mysticism is its mystery. I shall explain later how it came to have this unfortunate designation.

Among careful students of the subject there is no single, universally agreed upon definition. Another classic treatment, still relevant and useful after three-quarters of a century, is *Christian Mysticism* by William Ralph Inge who was the Dean of St. Paul's when the book was first published as his Bampton Lectures in 1899. In its appendix he gave twenty-six definitions of mysticism by various authors. Yet nearly a half-century later, when in 1947 Dean Inge summed up his lifetime of study of the subject in *Mysticism in Religion,* he disclaimed the need of such elaborate and varied definitions. He put a profound matter as simply as it can be stated in these words:

> Mysticism means communion with God, that is to say with a Being conceived as the supreme and ultimate reality. If what the mystics say of their experience is true, if they have really been in communion with the Holy Spirit of God, that is a fact of overwhelming importance, which must be taken into account when we attempt to understand God, the world, and ourselves.[4]

This I believe, and this is why the book is being written. But the term communion, and the distinctive elements of such communion to which the term mysticism may properly be applied, must be our next inquiry. We must also ask whether communion is the right word to use, since many definitions of mysticism put the emphasis on *union* rather than communion with the deity.

## 2. Communion or Union?

Rufus M. Jones has been my principal mentor in this field, for no one has done more to clarify the meaning and importance of mysticism. He was not only a devout Quaker but was long professor of philosophy at Haverford College, a man deeply committed to the service of humanity and the securing of social change through such service rendered in justice and love. This combination of interests makes him unusually qualified to speak about mysticism and its meaning in the life of our times.

The definitions of mysticism differ somewhat from one to another in his many books, but all stay close to that which he first submitted in *Studies in Mystical Religion* in 1909. "I shall use the word mysticism to express the *type of religion which puts the emphasis on immediate awareness of relation with God, on direct and intimate consciousness of the Divine Presence. It is religion in its most acute, intense and living stage.*"[5] He also indicates repeatedly that mysticism roots in a conviction of the kinship of God and man, and a mutual, reciprocal relationship in which finite man without self-deception can experience the presence of the Infinite. While this relationship is constant and is grounded in the nature of existence, an experience may be termed mystical when the ordinary barriers are transcended in a luminous sense of the Divine Presence.

Rufus Jones was always careful to emphasize that mysticism is not limited to the abnormal or the spectacular. A favorite metaphor was our "amphibian" existence whereby we live in two worlds at once—the world around us and the world of the Spirit. I recall hearing him preach a moving sermon with its text taken from Revelation 1:9, 10, "I John, your brother . . . was on the island called Patmos on account of the word of God and the testimony of Jesus. I was in the Spirit on the Lord's day." Was Rufus Jones a mystic himself? In his writings he testifies to three deeply moving experiences which by almost any authentic classical definition could be termed mystical: as a young man in the decision about his life career by a sense of divine mission; as a father on board ship bound for England when he was to learn the next day of the death of his beloved little son; years later in a hospital as he was recovering from a serious automobile accident.[6] Yet for the greater part of his life he moved in the relatively even tenor of Christian living and service, guided by the Inner Light.

I do not know whether Rufus Jones ever deliberately rejected the second sentence of his basic definition. Perhaps not, for in *The Luminous Trail* published in 1947 a year before his death he reaffirms it. Yet in *The Radiant Life* published in 1944, he drops out this sentence and makes no reference in the definition to mysticism's being "religion in its most acute, intense and living stage." [7]

I find this omission preferable for two reasons. For one, mysticism is not the only route by which religion can be "acute, intense and living." For example, Rufus Jones's own activity in the founding and longtime chairmanship of the American Friends Service Committee, and his attempt to forestall a second world war by leading a Quaker delegation to Germany which faced the Gestapo at Hitler's headquarters, were experiences meriting these adjectives. But I question also whether mysticism has to be as exceptional an experience as these words suggest. Communion with God occurs in the inner life, and it can be deeply sustaining without being in any sense startling.

In mystical experience there is a personal encounter of the individual with his God. But what kind of encounter? Thus far we have spoken of communion, which does not erase all the mystery but does have a fairly common and manageable meaning. Yet most of the historic definitions of mysticism have used instead of it the word *union*, or the adjective *unitive*. Even so definitive a writer as Evelyn Underhill in her classic entitled *Mysticism* defines the mystic's goal as union with the Absolute.[8] This idea, though usually not in the language of idealistic philosophy, appears again and again in the writings of the mystics.

Do they really mean this? It depends on how union is understood. It is clear that the mystics have meant more than a psychological or ethical conformity of the human will to God's, though emphasis has been placed on purgation and purity of heart as the first round in the mystic's ladder of ascent toward the bliss of heaven. Purgation, illumination, union—this is the threefold journey of the *scala perfectionis* which culminates in the vision of eternity within time.

Dom Cuthbert Butler tries to ameliorate the pantheistic implications of a metaphysical union with Deity by saying that the Catholic mystics, even when they speak of the soul's absorption in God, insist that the soul retains its own individuality and full personality.[9] Yet as I read them, I am not sure they have always done so. The language used seems often to slide back and forth between the union which connotes a breaking down of all barriers in the immediacy of Divine Presence—and this might more accurately be termed communion—and an assumed ontological merging of the finite with the Infinite for a transient but ecstatic period. This latter strain, which goes back to Plotinus and Neoplatonism as it was introduced into Christianity through Augustine, hovers on the borderline of pantheism while endeavoring to retain belief in the personal God of biblical Christian faith.

We cannot eradicate from mystical literature this reference to union with the Deity. It appears again and again in the Christian devotional classics, though not usually with as clearly Neoplatonic language as in Meister Eckhart, who is often quoted as the typical Christian mystic. He made much of the divine Ground, or Spark, or Center, or Apex, or "Innermost Essence" or "Bottomless Abyss" in the soul of every man, and hence of the blessedness of the union of the human soul with the God who pervades all existence. "When the soul enters into her Ground, into the innermost recesses of her being, divine power suddenly pours into her." "In the Spark, or center of the soul, there occurs true union between the soul and God." "God is nearer to me than I am to my own self." "If the soul knew herself, she would know all things." "Where God is there is the soul, and where the soul is there is God." [10]

It is not alone in Christian or Western mysticism that we find statements like these. Mystical union through the identity of the God within and the God without—the divinity in the soul of every man and the divinity that is Absolute Being and the Ground of all being—is basic also to Oriental mysticism. It appears most clearly in the Vedanta or Hindu type from which much of the current interest in yoga is derived. Brahman is the universal deity, Absolute Reality beyond space, time, and causation; Atman is the God within the individual soul as immanent, eternal Self. Since Brahman and Atman are one, there is a clear path, albeit a difficult and costing one, to the union of the human soul with God through meditation and other works prescribed to fulfill the necessary conditions. This theology is summed up in the basic and hence oft-quoted Vedic phrase, *tat tvam asi*, "That art thou." To Aldous Huxley this is the root of what he calls, in an important book by this title, "the perennial philosophy." [11]

What is the modern Christian or religious seeker to do with these assumptions? Many would certainly accept as a worthy goal the desire of George Fox to "walk cheerfully over the world answering that of God in every person." [12] The Inner Light which is at the heart of Quaker mysticism is not something that comes and goes with a flickering existence, though its discernment may. The presence of God in all things, including the inner life of man, is consistent with a type of theism that affirms both the transcendence and the immanence of God. It is affirmed without pantheism in the panentheism of the process theology and other forms of contemporary religious thought.[13]

So far, so good. But is the human soul, or self, ever actually merged with God in such a manner as to lose its own identity, even for a transient moment? I cannot think so. It runs counter to all the basic structures of Christian theology to assume it. The basic doctrines of man's creation, judgment, and redemption through Christ, man's moral imperatives and responsible freedom, center in the unique identity of each human self. Communion with God through the presence of the Holy Spirit, with its fruits in spiritual refreshment, guidance, and strengthening—of this our faith assures us. When union is conceived in the sense of an immediate awareness of the divine Presence, this is open to us. Union as ontological or existential loss of human identity in the divine is not. In a later chapter we must examine this at greater length.

The union mysticism of the great devotional classics can still teach us something if we recognize that in most cases the metaphysical question was not raised. But, for ourselves, we shall avoid trouble if we stick to the language of communion. When "spirit with Spirit shall meet," God remains God and man remains man, with an "I-Thou" relation in which there is meeting without merging. This I believe to be the essence of mysticism, and with it of a devotional life that is deep, strong, and life-sustaining.

Not everything that is called "devotions," whether it is a bit of private spiritual reading, the devotions with which it is customary to open a women's church meeting, or even the professionally led worship of Sunday morning, is a devotional experience. Still less is it a mystical one. Deep spiritual communion is rare, and costs more of us than we are usually willing to give. The devotional practices mentioned above ought not to be abandoned or disparaged if their mood and content are appropriate, for they assist not only in maintaining religious habits but in keeping within speaking distance of something deeper. Yet full communion with God involves a self-giving that claims the entire person, thinking, feeling, willing, and doing. The practice of the presence of God is no easy matter and extends not only to occasional periods but to all of life. Yet the humble and the mighty, the saints of the earth in whom is God's delight (Psalm 16:3), and the rest of us ordinary folk, can have it if we will.

## 3. Affirmation or Negation?

Another basic distinction as to the meaning of mysticism, related to the preceding but not identical with it, must now be indicated. Is mysticism essentially a negation or affirmation of the human self? To consider this we must take a glance at the early history of mysticism, and in doing so we shall see how mysticism got its name.

It is a mistake to suppose that the essence of mysticism is penetration of the mystery of the Infinite. Yet historically it has a connection with this objective that it has never entirely lost.

In the first centuries of the Christian era, the Greek and Roman world was full of mystery cults of various types, esoteric groups in which only the initiates had a secret knowledge of deity, or *gnosis,* which was denied to others. Gnosticism was one of these, and an early rival of Christianity. It had about it a pre-Christian Oriental mysticism in which it was assumed that the possessor of its secret knowledge would secure very special blessings in this life and the next. It gathered enough accretions from early Christianity to make of it something of a blend between the mystery religions and Christian faith. For this reason Gnosticism was viewed as endangering the true faith and was condemned as heretical.

Some experiences are recorded in the New Testament which might now be termed mystical, and there are passages, particularly in the letters of Paul and the Gospel of John, that easily lend themselves to this interpretation. Paul's conversion experience may have been of this nature. Paul and some of the authors of the other letters had much to say about the mystery of the gospel of Christ.[14] Such biblical foundations of Christian mysticism will be examined in the next chapter. Yet nowhere in the New Testament do we find a word that could be translated as mysticism. Among the church fathers, "contemplation" was the usual term to designate what was later to be called mystical experience.

However, toward the end of the fifth century a writing appeared which was entitled *Mystical Theology,* thus adopting a terminology made familiar by the mystery religions. The term lasted, and it is with us today. The author of this work claimed to be Dionysius the Areopagite, Paul's convert in Athens as recorded in Acts 17:34. It is certain that he was not this person, but as was common in those days without the stigma now attached to plagiarism he adopted a pseudonym to gain credence for his writing. For lack of knowledge of his real name he has to be called Pseudo-Dionysius, or simply Dionysius.

The main thrust of the *Mystical Theology* was the complete negation of the natural man's knowledge of God. The author's position is that God is completely transcendent, beyond all human thought, reason, intellect, or any approaches of the mind. A term which occurs repeatedly in this writing is "the Divine Dark." The human mind can only say what God is not, never what God is. There is nothing within the human self to give us any clue. But is there no way to penetrate this divine darkness? Yes, there is one. This is the *via negativa* by which the soul strips off its selfhood and, in ecstatic union with transcendent deity, both *feels* and *knows* its oneness with the Infinite.

This was to become a classic pattern of Christian mysticism. The "divine dark" appears in its full intensity in the anonymous English mystical writing *The Cloud of Unknowing* of the fourteenth century, which is a rather close replica of the mystical theology of Dionysius, and the first in English literature. Yet there are numerous indications elsewhere of this general point of view. While Dionysius gave this interpretation of mysticism its lasting name, Plotinus two centuries earlier had said something quite similar. Try as man will to lift his mind up to knowledge of the Infinite, he must then use "wings of flight," and Plotinus sums up this leap beyond human experience as "the flight of the alone to the Alone." Plotinus was not a Christian theologian but a Roman philosopher originally from Alexandria who believed that to say anything definite about God was to limit him, and Augustine in his earlier years before his conversion absorbed much of this line of thought.

In his mature thought and writing Augustine believed that we could know God through his revelation in Christ, but he never lost the sense of the immediacy of the vision of God beyond the reaches of the human intellect. In one of the most familiar and beautiful passages in mystical literature, he tells in his *Confessions* of a holy moment in deep fellowship with his mother Monica at the port of Ostia on their way back to North Africa from Milan, shortly before her death:

> And when our discourse was brought to that point, that the very highest delight of the earthly senses, in the very purest material light, was, in respect of the sweetness of that life, not only not worthy of comparison, but not even of mention; we raising up ourselves with a more glowing affection towards the "Self-Same," did by degrees pass

through all things bodily, even the very heaven, whence sun and moon, and stars shine upon the earth; yea, we were soaring higher yet, by inward musing, and discourse, and admiring of Thy works; and we came to our own minds, and went beyond them, that we might arrive at that region of never-failing plenty, where Thou feedest Israel for ever with the food of truth.[15]

"We came of our own minds, and went beyond them." This note is continued as he speaks of how the tumult of the flesh, the images of earth, and the very soul were hushed to "hear His Very Self without these, as we two now strained ourselves, and in swift thought touched on that Eternal Wisdom, which abideth over all."

Other mystics, whose grasp of the total sweep of Christian faith was less comprehensive than Augustine's, made much of this *via negativa*. It is a somewhat slippery term. Sometimes it is used to indicate an emphasis on the negation of self-centeredness and of reliance on human powers in contrast with faith and utter surrender to the call of God. One must curb "the I, the me, the mine" with its ever-present demands.[16] The negative way then blends with the affirmation type as an emphasis on the need of self-conquest in the love and service of God. Historically, however, it means more than that, with its goal the obliteration of selfhood in ecstatic union with God. To this there is often linked a disparagement of the human capacity to know God save by the mystical vision, and to this end the need of rigorous disciplines of prayer, fasting, prolonged meditation, and ascetic living.

In its historical setting, the *via negativa* roots in an understanding of God as utterly transcendent to human knowledge and thus inaccessible through ordinary approaches. This originated in Oriental thought, was brought into the Western tradition through Plotinus, and was mediated to Christianity through Plotinus and Dionysius. Rufus Jones calls this type of mysticism devotion to an "abstract Infinite" in contrast with the God of Christian faith whom we may know though Jesus Christ and whom we are called to love and serve with the affirmative use of all our powers.

What have been the fruits of the negative way? As seen frequently in Christian medieval mystics, these were not all bad. To the best of them God was no abstract figure, and their knowledge of God through the Christian gospel, with its call to love and serve him with their whole being, fended off what might have been more serious results in an esoteric distortion of the gospel. In some, the prolonged periods of fasting and contemplation withdrew them from normal human associations; in others, as with St. Francis, the conquest of self-love was accompanied by a joyous love of God and all God's creatures, whether bird, beast, or man. Not always but too often, the self-depreciation and "self-naughting" of the negative way encouraged an ascetic renunciation of wholesome bodily and social pleasures.

While I do not regard the negative way as either the sole type of experience that merits the term mystical or ordinarily the most desirable, it has its positive as well as its negative side. All Christian living that is more than casual requires self-denial, the purging of the soul by penitence, the renunciation of immediate pleasures at the call of love, the dedication of the self to the will of God at personal cost. In short, this cost is the way of the cross. The reward is God's acceptance and an ensuing holy joy. This note underlies all authentic Christian mysticism, for there is a "dying into life" which underlies Christianity. This note the exponents of the negative way have often stressed, to their own great profit and to ours if it is taken seriously, but it is not their exclusive prerogative.

The distinctions we have drawn between two major types of mysticism did not originate with Rufus Jones. They are deeply imbedded in discussions of mysticism that extend over the years. In 1926 Dom Cuthbert Butler, commenting on his own earlier work in this field, remarked, "I found that by . . . distinguishing between, on the one hand, 'acquired, active, ordinary contemplation,' and, on the other, 'infused, passive, extraordinary,' I had unwittingly plunged into the thick of the fray." [17] He cites numerous authors who differ as to whether the first of these should be termed mysticism. His conclusion is that there is a middle ground between giving the term a too restricted or too loose connotation. So I believe. The extremes have dangerous pitfalls.

A great deal of historic mysticism has been a blend—sometimes an illogical but nevertheless a vital blend—of union and communion, of negation and affirmation both of the human self and of the personal God of Christian faith who is known through Jesus Christ. We must expect to find all kinds. In what follows I shall not try to draw a sharp line between the types except where the distinctions are so clear as to make this inevitable.

### 4. The Psychological Marks of Mystical Experience

Mysticism is obviously not all of one type. Yet if it is not amorphously to go off in all directions, it must have some distinguishing features. Accordingly, we must look at its psychological expressions to see what is characteristic of that form of human experience which may properly be termed mystical. There are some such marks, though their intensity and quality vary, and they are not limited to religion, or at least to religion in its usual understanding.

The most famous list of such marks of mystical experience was given many years ago by William James in his *Varieties of Religious Experience.*[18] It will be recalled that he stated as its four characteristic marks its *ineffability,* its *noetic quality,* its *transiency,* and its *passivity.* These will serve usefully as a basis from which to expand, diminish, or redefine it, all of which I believe in some measure should be done.

Is the mystic's experience ineffable in the sense that he can find no words to describe it? The answer is yes and no. The wealth of mystical literature indicates that many millions of words have been used in the attempt, at least, to describe it. The fact that it is still talked about shows that the attempts were not wholly futile. Yet most of these witnesses testify to an inexpressible joy and peace—a state of being in the soul which words can only faintly adumbrate. This may well be akin to what Paul had in mind when he wrote from a Roman dungeon to the church at Philippi about "the peace of God, which passes all understanding."

William James defined the noetic quality by saying that mystical experiences "are states of insight into depths of truth unplumbed by the discursive intellect." In short, mystical experience adds to the subject's grasp of reality by an intuitive rather than a logical approach. It is not by sensory experience, scientific verification, or logical deduction that the mystic's knowledge is deepened, but by a clearer vision and a depth of feeling that seem to come from a Source beyond himself. This is why in Christian mysticism so strong an emphasis is laid on the love of God.

I believe this stress on insight and intuition and the discovery of something that seems to be given from without is a true description, though it has dangers if it is not safeguarded. It is in keeping with the word recorded in John 14:26, "But the Counselor, the Holy Spirit, whom the Father will send in my name, he will teach you all things." It is consistent also with much of the stress in modern existentialism on feeling as a surer guide than the intellect. Yet such a vision of God as the mystic experiences must be tested, not analytically while it is in process but in retrospect as one moves back to the light of every day, by its coherence with all the factors in human living which can be discerned through other channels.

The transiency of the mystical experience, at least in its more extreme forms, is unmistakable. No one can live "on the mountaintop" all the time. Such a form of mysticism requires the expenditure of a large amount of emotional energy, and to maintain it for long periods, even if one could do so, would be psychologically disruptive, easily merging into psychosis. In the milder forms of mysticism, in which one quietly endeavors to live in the presence of God with recurrent periods of spiritual refreshment, there is no such peril. But is this mysticism? The fact that there is no sharp dividing line between affirmation mysticism and consistent Christian living need not eliminate its reality as mystical experience if it centers in a direct and immediate experience of the presence of God.

Is passivity a mark of mysticism? Again one must say yes and no. Some mystical experiences seem to come unbidden. But after preparation. There is nothing passive about the endeavor to quiet one's mind and conflicting emotions so that one can hear the voice and feel the presence of God. So difficult is it to do this with any thoroughness that most of us do not even make the effort, whatever our so-called devotions. Yet the fruit of this effort can be the assurance that one does not have to carry his burdens alone. God will not solve all our problems for us, or exempt us from responsibilities of thinking and acting that one ought to carry. Yet as Alfred North Whitehead put it in enduring words, "God is the Great Companion, the fellow-sufferer who understands." [19] This the mystic most steadfastly believes, and while he may say it in other words he finds in this confidence a resting-place for his soul. Receptivity is the prerequisite of spiritual energy.

This analysis of the characteristic marks of mystical experience, which has deservedly become a classic, says much that is useful and important. Yet these four categories of William James do not cover the matter. In spite of a common center there are wide variations among the mystics, and each must be seen as a personal self with a life-style of his own. These individual life-styles and their contributions must be our concern later.

When Thomas Kepler some years ago compiled his massive and very valuable anthology of Christian devotional literature, he shed much light upon these varied mystical life-styles, though he did not use this term. Instead, he entitled the book *The Fellowship of the Saints.*[20] And what is a saint? Not, certainly, the model of moral rectitude commonly ascribed to this term in popular usage. Nor is a saint necessarily a person who has been officially canonized by the church. Nevertheless, difficult as the term is to define, it stands for something recognizable in a person's living—in his thinking and feeling, his speaking and acting, and sometimes in his writings about God, his fellowman, and himself. In the devotional writers of the past whose works have lasted, there is a quality of steadfast reliance on God, concern for others, a deep humility and absence of self-seeking, a staying-power and heroic singleness of purpose that enabled them to confront opposition and not quail before it, and in spite of times of deep suffering to find luminous joy in God and his creation. Some of them, especially of the *via negativa* tradition, were ascetics, and nearly all of them lived in outward simplicity. Yet for the most part without renouncing the sacraments of the church, they viewed all of life as sacramental. Such qualities, manifest in varying degrees and in many forms, are central to the mainstream of Christian mysticism.

### 5. Ecstasy and Objectivity

Two aspects of mystical experience, which are both psychological and theological in their rootage, call for special consideration.

Ecstasy is often said to be the climactic element in mystical experience, and we must inquire what this is. At the opposite extreme from this poignant subjectivity, the skeptical tenor of today's world often prompts the question whether mystical experience has any objective ground.

The term ecstasy is derived from the Greek *ekstasis,* a "standing out from." Though it need not always have a religious connotation, when applied to mysticism it suggests a withdrawal from everything in the normal self, and hence the *via negativa.* My dictionary defines ecstasy as "a state in which the mind is carried away as it were from the body; a state in which the functions of the senses are suspended by the contemplation of some extraordinary or supernatural object." It is a kind of "out of this world" rapture which is characteristic of the more extreme forms of mysticism.

Mystical ecstasy, sometimes regarded as being all there is of mysticism, must be examined from two angles. One is its place in the traditional threefold ascent of the mystic from purgation through illumination to union with the divine. The other is its possible connection with such psychological experiences as the trance, self-hypnosis, and the visions and voices which the psychologist is prone to regard as hallucinations.

Purgation to the mystic is a necessary first step, and a costing one, toward the unitive life in God. It calls for rigorous self-examination, penitence, and the endeavor to live blamelessly in the sight of God. It centers in the promise affirmed in the Beatitudes, "Blessed are the pure in heart, for they shall see God." The illumination stage involves contemplation, or in modern terminology meditation, and as a consequence the mystics of the past were often called contemplatives. It was commonly accompanied by fasting and long seasons of prayer, and by various disciplines of which the most famous are Ignatius Loyola's "Spiritual Exercises."

Union with God, we noted, has been variously conceived. A frequent though not a universal feature was the mystical ecstasy in which, for a brief indescribable moment, all barriers seemed to be swept away and new insight supernaturally imparted as one gave himself over fully to the Infinite One. It is apparent that William James's four descriptive terms apply aptly to this experience. It may also be viewed as a fresh self-orientation in which all one's faculties are grouped about a new center, "piercing like a single flame the barriers of the sensual world." [21] A famous mystic has described something very like it, saying, "I know a man in Christ who fourteen years ago was caught up to the third heaven—whether in the body or out of the body I do not know, God knows. . . . And he heard things that cannot be told, which man may not utter" (II Corinthians 12:2, 4).

The mystical ecstasy may or may not be spiritually fruitful. Probably we had better say that this depends on its accompaniments in the daily life of the person who experiences it.

However, we have noted another term which is much more common, both in the New Testament and in other Christian literature, which carries the values of ecstasy without its problems. This is *joy*. Joy is the accompaniment of any genuine mysticism, though it is far more than a superficial celebration of life, and, unlike pleasure, joy can be present even in deep suffering. We are told that Jesus said to his disciples even as he faced toward the agony of the cross, "These things I have spoken to you, that my joy may be in you, and that your joy may be full" (John 15:11). A later writer tells us that Jesus himself "for the sake of the joy that lay ahead of him, endured the cross, making light of its disgrace" (Hebrews 12:2 NEB).

Other terms for the feeling-tone that normally accompanies mystical experience are the "radiant" life and "luminous" character of the mystic way. Rufus Jones used each of these terms as titles in books which he wrote in the last decade of his life. Eugene W. Lyman in *The Meaning and Truth of Religion* states as the prime characteristics of mystical experience its immediacy, its objectivity, and its luminousness.[22] These terms referring to the lighted life are appropriate, provided we do not expect them to connote an ever-smiling countenance. Perhaps we had better adapt a word from the prologue of John's Gospel, "In him was life, and the life was the light of men," and say of the Christian mystic that in a special, though not in an exclusive, way he is called to be a bearer of that light.

This brings us to the matter of objectivity, the heart of the question from the standpoint of the relevance of mystical meditation in today's world. There are few persons who doubt that a deep religious experience, of which the mystical is one type, can alter an individual's outlook on himself and his world, normally for the better although sometimes in the opposite direction. Yet there are many persons who believe that such an experience is self-induced, welling up from the subconscious of the individual as the result of influences from without in conjunction with a complex set of internal forces including his own bodily states.

Yet mysticism presupposes objectivity, even if the God who speaks and discloses his presence is within. No mystic believes that he is "lifting himself by his own bootstraps," to cite a still useful cliché. If one believes this, or even seriously suspects it, he is no longer lifted. A large part of the religious world, to say nothing of the secular, is in this situation today.

Do we need to choose between objectivity, on the one hand, and a psychologically discernible subjectivity on the other? I believe this to be a false dichotomy. There is no sound reason to disparage the psychological study of mysticism or any other form of religious experience, provided it be recognized that psychology is not theology and had better not try to make pronouncements beyond its own sphere. If on sufficient theological or philosophical grounds one believes in the immanence of the transcendent God in all things, including the human body and spirit that constitute our selfhood, there is no insuperable barrier to the mystic's assurance of the divine Presence.

The grounding of this belief rests not in the mystical experience *per se*, but in the biblical witness to the living God, in the long tradition of the church, in personalistic philosophy,[23] and in a recognition that feeling and insight when tested by life as a whole provide a legitimate approach to truth. We shall conclude this chapter without spelling out all of these grounds, but we shall come to them again. Our next concern will be the biblical roots of mysticism, in which the existence of God and the possibility of knowing and meeting God through divine revelation are presupposed. But mysticism is more than a Christian phenomenon, even a "perennial" mode of conceiving the relation of the human spirit to the Ultimate Reality. Therefore we must inquire into its philosophical groundwork in a succeeding chapter. It seems best to leave the matter of its objectivity for further consideration until after these foundations can be canvassed.

# II

# Mysticism in the Bible

Since this book deals primarily with Christian mysticism, it is appropriate now to examine it roots in the Bible. The mystics and devotional writers of the past seldom made a fetish of the Bible, but directly or indirectly, they were nourished by it. Even without large personal acquaintance, as was the case in the Roman Catholic centrality of the Mass rather than the layman's personal access to the Bible, the encompassing ecclesiastical and liturgical climate had its rootage in Scripture. Within the Protestant domain there have been few, if any, great devotional writers to whom the Bible was not a precious heritage.

There is unquestionably a mystical note in the Bible, especially in the New Testament. Yet not everything that has religious or spiritual value is mystical. Where, then, are we to draw the line as we look at the Bible?

To review somewhat the preceding chapter, the basic note in mysticism is a direct and immediate awareness of the presence of God, whether in union or communion. Other characteristics in varying degrees and forms are associated with this center. Among them are fresh insights which the mystic believes come to him from beyond either sensory experience or logical deduction; an assurance of divine undergirding and support which becomes the more intense in especially luminous moments; and a joyous sense of the Divine Presence which at times seems to lift one out of his normal self and earthly entanglements, but which may also be experienced as a serene and steady confidence in the nearness and sufficiency of God.

Admittedly, mysticism is a slippery term, the more so because it is a highly individual experience, and individuals are not all run into one mold. Yet it has enough of a common center to be distinguishable from some other forms of religious experience. It is not primarily moralistic, nor liturgical, nor ecclesiastical, nor social activist, though there have been mystics with concerns along all of these lines, and in recent decades especially the last. It is not a theological system, though it has an implicit theological grounding. It is not an ethical system, though the mystics have always insisted that moral purity is a prerequisite to the vision of God and should also be its fruit. It stands at the opposite end of the scale from legalism, though most mystics have obeyed the laws of the land, of their church, and of the society around them unless they felt a strong impulsion of conscience to do otherwise. It is not nationally but individually oriented in its stance and outreach, yet there have been mystics who have exerted great influence in and upon their nations.

## 1. Mysticism in the Old Testament

Fortified with these affirmative and negative criteria as to what mysticism is, we must examine how it stands with mysticism in the Old Testament. We shall soon discover that in spite of its being a great source book of religion for both Jewish and Christian faiths, its dominant motifs are other than mystical.

It may be helpful to begin with an overview of Old Testament thought in its primary features and compare it with the main notes in the mystical outlook. This will be followed by a look at the various sections of the Old Testament.

The differences begin in the different way of conceiving the nature of God. To the Old Testament mind, God is the Creator, Judge, and Redeemer of men, the Lord of history, transcendent in his holiness and never to be identified with his created world. The mystic stresses the divine immanence to the point of sometimes skirting the edges of a monistic pantheism.

The Old Testament view of man makes him God's supreme creation, a responsible being made in the divine image and called to stewardship over nature. Yet man is a sinner; the Old Testament never lets us forget that, as Yahweh yearns to redeem his erring people. The mystics stress moral purity and the need of penitence, but because of the divine element within man as basic to his nature, they have usually taken a less bleak view of the human soul.

The Old Testament concept of the moral law is not wholly a legalistic compilation of codes of behavior, but it looks in this direction far more than is congenial to the mystic. On the other hand, the mystic is seldom antinomian, but he has more kinship with this position than the Hebrew mind could accept.

The basic theme of the Old Testament is God's movement in history. Destiny and doom are epitomized in the giving and the breaking of the covenant. The promised Messiah and the remnant whose fidelity will endure though the winnowing of time are important notes. To many mystics, though not all, the Eternal Now is a more congenial concept.

The faith of Israel as the chosen people makes it essentially a national religion. The mystic's union or communion with God occurs in individual persons, however related to one another in groups, and any corporate predestination is at variance with the universal love of God.

The main divisions of the Old Testament have traditionally been regarded as the books of history, law, and prophecy. To these modern scholarship adds wisdom literature and devotional poetry, with various subtypes of literature such as myth, apocalypse, and short stories interspersed. Only one of these has much in common with the mystical temperament. We must now ask why.

As for the historical narratives, the mystic lives in time, as all humanity must, and cannot be indifferent to the ongoing sequence of events in time. But this sequence, especially if it lies in the past, is not his main concern. Even in the present, he is sometimes charged with not having enough concern with what goes on around him! Yet time is a dominant note in Old Testament thought. It is to pillory the mystic too severely to say that that he thinks only of eternity and not of time, yet there is some ground for this charge. Most of the Christian mystics have believed in eternity as personal survival after death, but their greater concern, since they have entrusted the future to God, has been with eternal life in the Johannine sense as the blessedness of life in God here and now.

The law codes of the Hebrews have held little interest for the mystics. It is obvious that they share this disinterest with many others. There are great values in the books of the law as social artifacts, but few of the mystics have been sociologists of religion, whether past or present. It is clear that the detailed codes of conduct for an ancient day could not be the mystic's chief delight.

One might expect to find a closer affinity between the mystic's vision of God and the prophet's "Thus saith the Lord . . . ." Both are experienced as forms of revelation, the imparting of wisdom not of man's conjuring up. Yet there is an important difference between these two kinds of divine disclosure. The prophet proclaims to the people that which he believes Yahweh requires of them if they are to mend their evil ways and find favor in his sight. The mystic looks to God in praise and prayer and hopes for a vision of God that will enable him to live more fruitfully and faithfully. He is concerned with other people through his love of God, but he does not usually think of himself as God's spokesman with a message to deliver to a major group in society. Rabbi Abraham Heschel, who combines mystical and prophetic concern to a rare degree in today's world, states the difference in these words:

> Unlike the mystic experience, the significance of prophecy lay not in those who perceived it but in those to whom the word was to be conveyed. . . . The purpose was not in the perception of the voice but in bringing it to bear upon the reality of the people's life. Consequently, the substance of prophecy was in the content rather than in the act, and revelation was a prelude to action.[1]

This is not to say that the mystic finds nothing in the books of prophecy in the Bible. There are great soul-stirring passages in them, such as Isaiah 6, 40, or 53, which are themselves among the great devotional literature of the ages. Yet it is not in prophetic invectives against Israel's disobedience to the covenant with God, but in the vision of a new covenant in the hearts of men as set forth in Jeremiah 31:31-34 that the mystic finds his primary hope and challenge.

A related difference between Old Testament prophecy and the mystical temperament lies in the fact that the former was directed primarily to the nation as a corporate group that had broken its covenant and was trying to curry favor with the Almighty by external forms and ceremonies. The mystic likewise protests the substitution of ceremony for inner reality and enjoins holy obedience, but this is mainly a matter between the individual and his God.

As for the wisdom literature, the mystics have struggled with the mystery of evil as did Job, but never have been much concerned to deal with the problem of evil theologically or to construct a theodicy. Suffering has for the most part been accepted as part of God's mysterious providence, with this same providence enabling one to live triumphantly and even joyously in spite of pain. Suffering thus viewed becomes a form of chastening to the soul, but not a curse.

Still another difference emerges in the majestic closing chapters of Job. When the Voice speaks from the whirlwind to rebuke Job for his human presumption and to assert the power of the Almighty over all nature, what is being stressed is the transcendence of the Creator over his total created world, not his immanent presence within it. This is the dominant Old Testament stance. Here the mystical experience is ambivalent. Early mysticism, particularly of the *via negativa* type, made much of the utter transcendence of God. This gradually gave way to a greater recognition of the presence of the divine within the human spirit. Western mysticism, at least until recent times, has not questioned that God in his holiness is more than man or nature; yet it is his presence, not his otherness, that is most congenial to the mystical temper.

Neither the moral platitudes of the book of Proverbs, however pungently stated, nor the hedonism of Ecclesiastes imported from the Greek world, is very consonant with the mystical temperament. This is too obvious to require elaboration. This leaves for consideration among the Old Testament books only the Song of Solomon and the Psalms.

Of the Song of Solomon it must be said that some of the mystics, most notably Bernard of Clairvaux, made much of it as an allegorical presentation of the love of God. In their rapture at being caught up in the divine embrace the mystics more than once failed to distinguish sharply between human erotic love and the love of God. As the psychologists are wont to remind us, the fact of being celibates immured in a cloister with no normal sexual outlets for their fantasies may have added to this tendency. I believe it unfair to charge that this was or is a primary characteristic of the mystical temperament. Yet it has undoubtedly at times been present, and the Song of Solomon was a ready justification for "spiritual marriage." [2]

Before biblical scholarship had discerned that this romantic poem was a Hebrew love song designed to be sung at weddings, and not an allegorical prophecy of the coming of Christ as the Bride of the Church, it lent itself readily to distortion. A distinguished scholar in the field of mysticism, Dean Inge, says this of it:

> A graceful romance in honour of true love was distorted into a precedent and sanction for giving way to hysterical emotions, in which sexual imagery was freely used to symbolise the relation between the soul and its Lord. Such aberrations are as alien to sane Mysticism as they are to sane exegesis.[3]

Of all the Old Testament books, it is in Psalms that the mystic finds himself most at home. The psalms have many themes—the transcendent holiness of God, the rewards of moral righteousness, the call to repentance and cleansing from sin, the praise of nature as God's handiwork. Even though some of these are not the mystic's primary emphasis, they are couched in the language of deep devotion, and the mystic's mood is that of praise and prayer. Yet the notes most central to his main concern are also to be found in the psalms—the thirst of the soul for God, the affirmation of security in God's almighty care, the guidance of God's hand, the intimate nearness of the divine as the guardian and sustenance of the soul.

This book of devotion, a compilation of poetry which served as the hymnbook of the second Temple long centuries ago, never wears out. Through many changes in the human social situation, including those of our own times, it continues to nourish the heart of man. While contemporary worship may add new elements, it cannot replace it. Many passages could be cited as illustrating why the mystics have loved the psalms, but one will suffice. It would be difficult to find a more perfect description of a direct and immediate awareness of the presence of God than is found in these words:

> Whither shall I go from thy Spirit?
> Or whither shall I flee from thy presence?

If I ascend to heaven, thou art there!
If I make my bed in Sheol, thou art there!
If I take the wings of the morning
and dwell in the uttermost parts of the sea,
even there thy hand shall lead me,
and thy right hand shall hold me.
(Psalm 139:7-10)

## 2. The Synoptic Gospels

The tenor of the first three Gospels is not primarily mystical, though mystical elements are to be found in them. What they do is to present in narrative form the memories and oral tradition connected with the birth, baptism, ministry, death, and resurrection of Jesus, with extensive accounts of his teachings interspersed. A vast amount of New Testament scholarship has gone into the study of the extent to which these narratives and the presentation of the words of Jesus are historically authentic. We cannot go into these questions here, but must look at the records as they stand to see what there is in them that reflects the mystical temper. This gives some indication of the extent to which the Christian devotional writers have used Matthew, Mark, and Luke as their sources.

We find, in the first place, that the cardinal foundation of authentic mystical experience—that the vision of God comes to the pure in heart—is stated by Jesus in the Sermon on the Mount. Whether it is *only* the pure in heart who shall see God is a matter of variable interpretation, especially since Paul had his ecstatic conversion experience at the very beginning of his Christian life with a background of what then is recognized as evildoing. However, in classical Christian mysticism there has been no question that purity of heart is demanded of the soul that would seek an intimate sense of divine Presence. It would have seemed an utter travesty of spiritual worship to induce it through drugs or by such physical or mental exercises as might of themselves produce an ecstatic trance. This says something of importance to the mysticism of today.

The indwelling presence of God or of Christ appears in a number of passages in the Synoptics. Before the newer translations had made us aware that Luke 17:21 says, "The kingdom of God is in the midst of you," the older rendering of "The kingdom of God is within you" was often quoted as evidence of the presence of God in the human soul. A similar implication with Christ as God is drawn from such passages as "Where two or three are gathered in my name, there am I in the midst of them" (Matthew 18:20), and "Lo, I am with you always, to the close of the age." (Matthew 28:20). Here the clear implication of divine presence has survived the translation process.

Many supernatural events are to be found in the narrative materials, and most of these reflect the writer's sense of wonder at the works of Jesus. These are scarcely within the orbit of mysticism. Two scenes in particular, however, have a mystical tinge and savor. These are the phenomena connected with the baptism of Jesus and his transfiguration in the presence of Peter, James, and John. Neither is a clear instance of mystical ecstasy, but in the one the voice from heaven with the visible descent of the Spirit of God, and in the other the supernatural light illumining the face of Jesus and the evident joy of the disciples, look in the direction of a mystical experience. So do the resurrection experiences, but this is so complex an issue that it would carry us considerably afield to try to assess them.

Was Jesus a mystic? There seems no doubt that he often spent times of deep communion with the Father. We are told little of these times of prayer except the agony in Gethsemane, but they were doubtless consistent in tenor with the prayer he taught his disciples, and were directed to his own sense of need in the furtherance of his mission. There is no question that Jesus felt a deep sense of kinship with the Father and had an intimate sense of divine presence which actuated his ministry and teaching. Indeed, his cry of desolation from the cross shows how much this sense of Presence meant to him.

Nevertheless, I do not think we can say that Jesus was a mystic. These mystical elements are present, but he cannot be run into a single category. He had every gift of the mystic, but more. Let us not make him the exemplar of our own main concern, whether this be big business,[4] social activism, or any other pursuit. If we are to try to classify such a universal man, he is best viewed, not as a mystic, but as a prophet of Israel and a rabbinical teacher with a marvelously fresh and life-giving outlook on the nature of both God and man.

## 3. The Mysticism of Paul

It is in Paul that we find the first great Christian mystic. His mysticism is not in all respects typical but it is unmistakably present. The author of the Fourth Gospel also shows clear evidences of mysticism, but we shall begin with Paul because he wrote nearly a half-century earlier.

It will be fruitful to examine Paul's mysticism from two angles, related but by no means identical: his unusual conversion experience and what came after it, with a word on his later visions,[5] and the meaning and theological foundations of his Christ-mysticism, or being "in Christ."

Paul's conversion is described three times in the book of Acts, in Acts 9:1-9; 22:6-11; and in 26:12-18. Furthermore, while the account in II Corinthians 12:2-4 is given in the third person, it is apparently autobiographical. Paul also refers to his vision of Christ at several points in the letters, particularly in I Corinthians 9:1; 15:8; Galatians 1:15-16, and perhaps also in II Corinthians 4:6. In these passages the details are not spelled out, but the implication is strong that Paul believed he had actually seen the risen Lord and had heard him speak.

Two features stand out with clarity in these passages: (1) that Paul regarded this conversion experience with its vision of Christ as the turning point in his life and the foundation of his calling and mission, and (2) that the phenomena connected with it are much like those of a mystical ecstasy. The sudden, blinding light, the voice, the sense of being "caught up into heaven" and of having heard "things that cannot be told, which man may not utter"—all this fits the mystical pattern in its more climactic forms. So does its cost in subsequent living. The main difference is that with Paul it stands at the beginning of his Christian life, while with the later Christian mystics the experience was more apt to occur further along the Christian way, as a kind of "second blessing" or as a fresh renewal of faith and dedication after years of being a Christian.

Because of these unusual elements in the record, it has been customary to say that Paul was smitten with epilepsy, or that he had a sudden traumatic attack of hysteria. Although he did have a persistent "thorn in the flesh" of which he does not reveal the nature, there is no evidence elsewhere of his having epileptic seizures. Furthermore, in view of the many hardships that he endured with fortitude and his calmness under crisis in the shipwreck, Paul does not seem like a man of neurotic temperament who would be apt to give way to a sudden spell of hysteria, even though "breathing threats and murder against the disciples of the Lord." It seems more plausible to say that his conscience had been goading him for some time, perhaps ever since Stephen with a face "like the face of an angel" had given his final witness as he was being stoned to death, and "the witnesses laid down their garments at the feet of a young man named Saul." (Acts 6:15–7:58.) With less famous persons than Paul, it has many times happened that what seemed like a sudden conversion was the result of long and deep stirrings in the subconscious mind which finally broke through into the conscious with overwhelming force.

If this is what happened on the Damascus road, there is no reason to dismiss it as "merely psychological." God works within the human spirit in both usual and unusual ways. He can be present in both normal and abnormal mental states, and "abnormal" does not need to have a pejorative meaning. Every genius is abnormal, and whatever may be thought of what happened in Paul's conversion, he was a religious genius whose letters and accomplishments bear witness to this fact.

It is not possible to give an exact analysis of Paul's spiritual development from this point forward; yet such evidence as we have in Acts and the letters give indications of it. Evelyn Underhill has traced these in *The Mystic Way*[6] and shows that they conform significantly to the sequence of spiritual growth found again and again among the mystics.

Following the traumatic upsurge of long-suppressed emotions which resulted in Paul's conversion, there is a period of withdrawal into Arabia. Like Jesus in the wilderness after his baptism, Paul needed to think through what had occurred, search out God's leading, and gather spiritual energy for what might lie before him. Then come the years of service at Antioch as a subordinate to Barnabas, a service of teaching that was useful but not much acclaimed, probably restrictive and humbling to Paul's restless spirit. In the language of mysticism this was a time of purgation. Only after the call to missionary service does

Saul become Paul and assume real leadership. Then, filled with the Holy Spirit, he spoke boldly for his faith.

An examination of his letters in the probable sequence of their writing shows development in Paul himself. In I and II Thessalonians the emphasis is on divine judgment and the need of penitence, interspersed with injunctions to fidelity while awaiting the Lord's coming. Purgation is still present. The next group, to the Corinthians, Galatians, and Romans, has Christ the Savior as its constant note, which indicates greater depth and spiritual maturity in Paul himself. In the mystical sequence this is a period of illumination. But not without its interruptions. There are not only "fightings without" but "fears within." The inner conflict so vividly described in Romans 7 and brought to glorious resolution in Romans 8 may refer, not to his conversion experience, but to something much nearer the time of this writing. Miss Underhill believes that he experienced "the dark night of the soul" but refused to give in to apathy. Then in Philippians, in Philemon, and in Colossians and Ephesians if he wrote them, the mystic's peace and joy through a constant sense of divine presence is visible. Paul was a great servant of God, but very human.

Much the same may be said of Paul's dramatic visions, as when he had a vision in the night of a man of Macedonia who was standing and beseeching him saying, "Come over to Macedonia and help us" (Acts 16:9-10). A dream? Perhaps. But he felt that the Lord was calling him, and he went with the result that the church at Philippi was founded. This was later to prompt his writing one of his most tender and faith-filled letters, which still nourishes our spirits today. It may well be that the vision—or the dream—was prompted by some previous thought of his venturing across the Bosporus into Europe, but this makes it no less the call of the Lord.

Yet these somewhat unusual experiences are not the primary ground for regarding Paul as the first great Christian mystic. This we should judge him to be from his letters even if he had never had any such visions.

It is generally acknowledged that Paul was the first great theologian of the church, and that he set the pattern for much that has lasted in Christian thought to the present. Yet his theology does not stem primarily from closely reasoned argument.

Nor is he interested in external evidences of the truth about God, as in the field usually termed apologetics. In part, Paul's theology shows the marks of his Jewish heritage, as in the sacrificial and atoning death of Christ for the sins of mankind. Yet in larger part it rests on the inner witness of the Spirit, which he had experienced and which he believed others should experience for the transformation of life. This tends to soften his doctrine of atonement and give fresh meaning to the death and resurrection of Christ. It is this note of inner witness, not conjured up from within but imparted through Christ, which is the groundwork for Paul's Christ-mysticism.

The bond between Paul's own conversion and his sense of the inner, yet Christ-imparted, authority of his message appears often in Paul's writing, but nowhere more clearly than in Galatians 1:11-12, "For I would have you know, brethren, that the gospel which was preached by me is not man's gospel. For I did not receive it from man, nor was I taught it, but it came through a revelation of Jesus Christ." This is followed directly by a reference to his own conversion and the resultant change in the orientation of his life.

This sense of direct relationship with Christ—not with the historic man Jesus whom Paul apparently never met personally, but with the risen Christ—never left him. To this primary note is added another, not the exclusive domain of the mystic but central to this mode of thought. This is the identification of the Holy Spirit with the Spirit of Christ. Paul appears to speak interchangeably of "the Spirit of God," or "the Spirit of Christ," or "the Spirit of Jesus Christ," or "the Holy Spirit," or simply "Christ" or "the Spirit." There was as yet no formal doctrine of the Trinity, but obviously such an identification was moving in this direction. The identification becomes complete when Paul says, "Now the Lord is the Spirit, and where the Spirit of the Lord is, there is freedom" (II Corinthians 3:17).

It is the Spirit, then, that becomes for Paul the ultimate criterion of truth and the ground of authority for the human spirit in both thought and action. Sometimes he calls it "the mind of Christ," which we are justified in relating to the ministry and teachings of Jesus, though if Paul does so it is not expressly stated. His usual term for the ultimate authority of the Christian is simply the Spirit. This is evident in such affirmations as, "For the Spirit searches everything, even the depths of God. . . . And we impart this in words not taught by human wisdom but taught by the Spirit, interpreting spiritual truths to those who possess the Spirit. . . . The spiritual man judges all things but is himself to be judged by no one" (I Corinthians 2:10-15).

It is but a short step from this identification of Christ with the Spirit, and then the placing of authority within the Spirit, to Paul's Christ-mysticism. The way of salvation is to be "in Christ." Paul uses this term more than thirty times in his letters, as any good concordance will indicate. The same thought is expressed in such words as "I have been crucified with Christ; it is no longer I who live, but Christ who lives in me" (Galatians 2:20); "For you have died, and your life is hid with Christ in God" (Colossians 3:3); "Here there cannot be Greek and Jew, . . . but Christ is all, and in all" (Colossians 3:11); "My little children, with whom I am again in travail until Christ be formed in you!" (Galatians 4:19). All such passages have a mystical implication which puts the emphasis on the Christ within the believer. This is summed up in the affirmation which directly follows Paul's statement that the Lord is the Spirit: "And we all, with unveiled face, beholding the glory of the Lord, are being changed into his likeness from one degree of glory to another; for this comes from the Lord who is the Spirit" (II Corinthians 3:18). No medieval mystic could have improved on this as a consummation of the *scala perfectionis!*

Yet the inward Christ is not all there is of Paul's thought. Paul makes much of dying and rising with Christ; in short, of dying into life. This is the centuries-old doctrine of sacrificial atonement, but shorn of its legalism, internalized, and made relevant to the individual person. It hinges on the external, historical fact of the death and resurrection of Christ for man's redemption. Yet Paul's essential contribution is that through Christ's dying and rising, something akin to it may occur in every man for the transformation of the life of the believer. It is this dying into life, rather than the rebirth accented in John's Gospel, which is focal to Paul's thought as he writes, "Therefore, if any one is in Christ, he is a new creation; the old has passed away, behold, the new has come" (II Corinthians 5:17).

This facet of Paul's thought is, of course, not an exclusive prerogative of mysticism. Yet it has long been prized by the mystical temperament, not primarily as a doctrine but as a mode of being and a manner of living. It has enabled the mystic to undergo suffering, whether of physical or mental pain, social ostracism, or "the dark night of the soul," and to come out victoriously on the far side of it with a more vital sense of the Christ within. It is a primary source of the luminous and radiant life and the staying power amid difficulties which were earlier referred to as dominant characteristics of the saint.[7]

A further word should be added about the basis of Paul's mysticism. It is sometimes said that it is connected with the universality of the divine in every man recorded in Acts 17:22-31 as the central note in Paul's address in the Areopagus at Athens. I doubt that this claim can properly be made. In the first place, for the Athenians to have an altar "to an unknown god" would be contrary to the basic tenets of Greek thought, which believed in many gods but had no monotheism of this type. The inscription could have read "to the unknown gods" but hardly to one.[8] Furthermore, up to the final words which speak of judgment through Christ and assurance of this to all men through his resurrection from the dead, the passage is straight Stoicism. It was Stoic thought, not the Judaism in which Paul had been reared, which affirmed that God has "made from one every nation of men to live on all the face of the earth," and that "in him we live and move and have our being . . . for we are indeed his offspring" (Acts 17:26, 28). Paul's major emphasis through the letters is that it is in Christ, and not by nature, that all distinctions of race and culture are overcome, and it is in Christ, and not by birth, that we become sons of God.

What then shall we do with this passage? It affirms a great truth, later incorporated into an important strand of Christian thinking. Yet as far as Paul is concerned, we had better not regard this passage as a basis of his mysticism.

A second observation is somewhat related to this one. It is being-in-Christ rather than being-in-God that is central to Paul's thought, hence his Christ-mysticism. This is not an absolute distinction, for to Paul, Christ is the mediator between God and man and the Spirit of God is the Spirit of Christ. Either God or Christ may be spoken of as Lord. Yet the emphasis still centers in Christ, and we find in Paul's words no such repeated call to be "in God" as to be "in Christ." This means that the transcendent God of Hebrew faith is still the high and holy one, though no longer the God of Israel only, for in Christ those who were far off have now been brought near.

To sum up, to be in Christ connotes for Paul both an internal and an external relationship, each indispensable to the other and vital to the Christian believer. From one angle, to be in Christ means that Christ as the Spirit of God is within the Christian, addressing, guiding, comforting, rebuking, forgiving, strengthening him for life's tasks. Yet the Spirit is never an amorphous something that might be identified with the believer himself. Christ is the incarnate Lord, who had lived, died, risen again, and returned to the Father, yet as Spirit still lives eternally. To be in Christ, then, is to live a transformed life in faith, hope, and love through the enabling grace of this incarnate, indwelling Christ. Paul states it perfectly in the cryptic words, "I am crucified with Christ: nevertheless I live; yet not I, but Christ liveth in me" (Galatians 2:20 KJV). A mystery? Yes. But an actuality in Paul's life, and in that of many others.

## 4. The Gospel of John

Although Paul was the first great Christian mystic, the author of the Fourth Gospel produced what has been termed "the charter of Christian Mysticism." [9] It contains no such analysis as was later to appear in the *Mystical Theology* of Pseudo-Dionysius, but the mystical spirit pervades it. Clement of Alexandria in the third century called it "the spiritual Gospel," and this it has seemed to uncounted numbers since that time.

The power of this Gospel to move the reader to a deeper spiritual life has outlasted the changes brought about by historical and textual study. It was present when it was believed for centuries to be the work of John the beloved disciple, and it still persists when generally regarded by biblical scholars as the work of an unknown Christian writer toward the close of the first century of the Christian era. This person, whoever he was, was a man of deep spiritual insight who, in a historical framework less accurate than the Synoptics, caught the meaning of Christ in relation to both God and the human spirit.

This meaning he was able to put into imperishable words. From radical differences in style and purpose it is clear that he was not the John who wrote the book of Revelation. However, it is probable that the John of the Gospel wrote at least the first of the Epistles of John, and from the angle of mysticism I John and the Gospel of John carry a common outlook.

While a mystical spirit pervades this writing, it is not easy to pin it down to specific words, and it appears more clearly in some portions of the writing than in others. We shall look at it not sequentially but topically. The main topics will be the author's understanding of God, Christ, and the Holy Spirit; his concept of rebirth and eternal life in the present; his use of symbolism; and the bearing of all of these on the life of the Christian believer. These are so intertwined that there is overlapping.

In John's Gospel, God is not only the Father of Christ who is everywhere designated as the Son, but God is Love, God is Light, God is Spirit. This is affirmed with a corresponding suggestion of what is required of the Christian. "He who does not love does not know God; for God is love" (I John 4:8). "God is light and in him is no darkness at all. If we say we have fellowship with him while we walk in darkness, we lie and do not live according to the truth; but if we walk in the light, as he is in the light, we have fellowship with one another" (I John 1:5-7). "God is spirit, and those who worship him must worship in spirit and truth" (John 4: 24). Yet these attributes of God are not simply abstract qualities; they are very personal. God is not just another name for the presence of these qualities in human persons, as the humanism or radical immanentism of the present tends to affirm. God is the supreme personal being who has not only made all things, but who continues to love, enlighten, and inspire. This same God has become incarnate in Christ, who manifests in his own person the love of God, the light of the world, and the eternal divine Spirit.

This concept of God undergirds the entire writing. We find here no expressly stated doctrine of the Trinity, but the groundwork is laid for one. We noted this to be true in Paul's letters. There is, however, a difference. While John like the other Gospel writers tells the story of the crucifixion and resurrection of Jesus, it is on the incarnation rather than the death of Jesus that the emphasis is laid. In the Son is the full manifestation of the love of God, but also of the power and the wisdom of God.

This explains why in John, far more than in the Synoptics, Jesus appears always to be in full command of every situation. There is no agony in Gethsemane, or cry of dereliction from the cross. He is opposed and eventually is betrayed and crucified, but every incident is a witness to God's power and to Christ's own as God's representative. Thus he can not only perform such miracles as turning water into large amounts of wine and walking on the surface of the sea, but he can raise Lazarus from the dead. Yet, at the same time, Jesus is human. He experiences hunger, thirst, and weariness; he can feel such emotions as anger, sorrow, and disappointment. Such references, though apparently incidental, are important, for the narrative is throughout a witness to the real incarnation of God within the human, historical scene.

This implicit theme becomes explicit in the prologue of the Gospel, and Jesus here, and not again later, is called the Word, or Logos. He is the eternal, divine, cosmic Christ, God's agent in creation and the life and light of the world; yet he has become a man to share our human experience. "And the Word became flesh and dwelt among us, full of grace and truth; we have beheld his glory, glory as of the only Son from the Father. . . . And from his fullness have we all received, grace upon grace" (John 1:14-16). In these words are epitomized not only the incarnation, but the heart of Christian mystical experience. The mystic's life and light, his spiritual strength, and his capacity to love God and his fellowman, come to him from a divinity that is beyond, yet manifest within, the world of human experience.

The unity of Christ with the Father, presupposed throughout, comes to explicit expression again in the Last Supper discourse, and especially in the seventeenth chapter where he pleads for the unity of his followers with one another on the ground of his oneness with the Father. His prayer is "that they may all be one; even as thou, Father, art in me, and I in thee" (John 17:21). How shall we understand these words? As an ontological identity of being? Or as a unity of thought, of will, and of service in love? The latter seems the more plausible answer in view of the inevitable plurality of human existence. Yet there is a great ground of trust and confidence and a great challenge to Christian living in the awareness that the same divine Spirit who was in Christ is within us also.

The author makes it clear that it is through the Spirit that regeneration takes place. This is apparent in the encounter with Nicodemus in John 3:1-15. How does this occur? It is a mystery, like the blowing of the wind, but by the wind (or breath) of the Spirit it comes to pass. The same thought is present also in the story of Jesus and the Samaritan woman at the well in chapter four.

However, the major attention to the Spirit in this Gospel is found in the farewell discourse, where the promise of the Paraclete is given (John 14:16, 26; 15:26; 16:7). The Comforter-Counselor-Helper-Advocate (there is no single word in English that exactly says it) will come as the continuing witness to Christ, and as the Spirit of truth will be the guide and support of his followers. This promise takes the place in the Fourth Gospel of a note much more prominent in the Synoptics and Paul; namely, the imminent second coming of Christ himself.

The author's concepts of rebirth and of eschatology meet in his thought of eternal life as the present experience of the faithful believer. With the coming of Christ as the revealer of God and the savior of the world, the "age to come" is here. Judgment is at work in the here and now, and separation is taking place between those who will and those who will not accept the salvation available in Christ. "Truly, truly, I say to you, unless one is born anew, he cannot see the kingdom of God" (John 3:3). Yet salvation is available, for "God so loved the world, that he gave his only Son. . . ." And the Son offers this promise and extends this invitation, "He who hears my word and believes him who sent me, has eternal life; he does not come into judgment, but has passed from death to life" (John 5:24).

These words have traditionally been taken not only by the mystics but by many others as referring to the promise of eternal life beyond the physical death of the individual. This is not negated, and there is a brief passage in John 5:28, 29 which refers to a final resurrection. Millions of bereaved persons have been comforted by the promise found in John 14:1-3. Yet the meaning is clear. It is not only the hidden but assured life beyond death, it is the goodness, the glory, and the blessedness of life in Christ in the present that the author means by eternal life. And that is exactly what the mystics have sought and have found to their radiant joy.

We must conclude this survey with a look at the symbolism which abounds in John's Gospel. In part this is a symbolism of works, which are then interpreted as signs of the supernatural power and divine authority of Jesus. Yet there is a pointer in each toward a human relationship as well. There are eight miracles in the Gospel, and if we look at such accounts as the feeding of the five thousand, the healing of the man born blind, or the raising of Lazarus, it is not difficult to see that they speak, not solely of the God-given authority of Jesus, but of compassion for human need and service rendered in love.

There is also the meaningful symbolism of the "I am . . ." passages—pictorial metaphors that link divinity with humanity to serve our deepest needs. There are seven of these: "I am the bread of life" (6:35, 48) "I am the light of the world" (8:12); "I am the good shepherd" (10:11); "I am the door" (10:7); "I am the resurrection and the life" (11:25); "I am the way, and the truth, and the life" (14:6); "I am the true vine" (15:1, 5). Each carries its own great message which has provided spiritual guidance and support to Christians through the ages. They need not be elaborated, but the last, in particular, has a special bearing upon mysticism.

"I am the true vine, and my Father is the vinedresser. . . . I am the vine, you are the branches." No other passage in the entire Gospel affords such a direct expression of the mystical union between Christ and the Christian. It is a mistake to interpret it pantheistically, as is sometimes done, for there is no indication of a metaphysical merging of Christ and the disciple. Yet it affirms vividly both the presence of God in Christ and of the divine Spirit of Christ within his followers. Furthermore, it does so with a primary emphasis upon love, fruit-bearing, and an obedient, trust-filled abiding in Christ.

This passage sums up the major notes in the Fourth Gospel. Here we find epitomized the demands and fruits of an inward union with Christ and of outward service in his name. These are suggested in the utter dependence of the branch upon the vine for its nourishing; the need of prayer in conformity with the will of Christ, for only that kind is effective; the glorification of the Father, not in words only but by the life one lives; the primacy of love as the basic commandment; the fullness of joy which ensues from this relationship.

It is sometimes said that the mysticism of Paul centers in regeneration; that of John in incarnation. This distinction must not be pushed too far, for in both there is the message of coming to new life in Christ and of living in fellowship with Christ. Yet there is a difference. The blessedness of peace and joy in the divine presence for which Paul had to struggle and which appears in fullness only in his later writing seems from the beginning to pervade the spirit of this writer. Indeed, his "sense of the Presence" is the keynote of the book. This is why the mystics have loved it so much.

The new life in Christ, which the author presents with great artistry and insight, comes from loving companionship and obedience to Christ, the Son of the Father who has also called us to sonship. But not without cost! "See what love the Father has given us, that we should be called children of God; and so we are. . . . Beloved, we are God's children now; it does not yet appear what we shall be, but we know that when he appears we shall be like him, for we shall see him as he is. And every one who thus hopes in him purifies himself as he is pure" (I John 3:1-3). This love, this hope, and this self-purification through the Spirit have given vitality to Christian mysticism through the centuries.

# III

# Philosophical Grounds of Mysticism

In this chapter we shall survey the philosophical grounds, or foundations, of mystical experience from four angles. There is, first, the need to explore the basic presuppositions of mystical experience, taking into account the fact that while there are wide differences in types and among individuals, there are still some common presuppositions without which there would be no mysticism to talk about.

A second need is to explore the nature of ultimate reality as this is viewed in various types of mysticism. In particular, we must look at the interplay of pantheistic concepts in comparison with the assumptions of Christian theism.

A third approach to philosophical foundations lies in the exploration of its historical roots. The biblical bases of Christian mysticism were examined in the preceding chapter. These have predominated throughout the Christian mystical stream, but not without being strongly influenced at times by Greek philosophy. To see how this entered the Christian bloodstream we must give more attention to Plato, Plotinus, and Dionysius than was possible in a brief mention in the first chapter.

Fourth, there is the need to tackle more fully than previously the very vital question of the objectivity of the mystical experience. There is no question of the mystic's conviction of its objectivity; he is sure that he is in contact with a real Supreme Being that is more than and other than his own subjective mental states. But is this assumption a valid one?

All of these are large questions. Each could well merit a chapter—or a book—in itself. Yet there is a reason for looking at them together, for they dovetail into each other and there are factors in regard to each which throw light on the others.

## 1. The Mystic's Presuppositions

There can be no philosophy, and, indeed, no quest for truth in any field, without presuppositions. Mathematics has its axioms; science rests on the assumption of the orderliness of nature which makes possible a formulation of its laws. Presuppositions in any field determine the nature of the procedures that are followed in it. What then are the mystic's presuppositions?

The first of these is that the five senses are not the only approach to knowledge, or to other vital aspects of human living. The mystic is usually ready enough to admit that for most of our everyday world of experience, what we see, hear, taste, smell, and touch gives us the raw material which our minds interpret as knowledge of the world around us. Yet he does not believe that this is the only access to truth or to reality, for he does not believe that the material world is the only world there is.

This leads to a second presupposition—that there is a realm of the spirit which is related to the material world but is not identical with it. Whatever this may mean about its wider existence beyond man, this realm of the spirit is within man. The human spirit is able to do more than to respond to sensory impulses; it can think, feel, will, love, reflect upon itself, set goals beyond itself and pursue great objectives. Furthermore, says the mystic, the human spirit has the capacity to discern some kinds of truth through channels other than the ordinary ones of sensation and rational deduction. It uses these channels, to be sure, but finds in their use a deeper meaning. This may be called insight or intuition, even vision if one is careful not to mean by it some sort of hallucination. If the mystic is a Christian, he is apt to say with Paul that spiritual truths must be spiritually discerned. If he is not, he may say it in other words, but he still believes this to be true.

Thus far, we have two basic presuppositions of the mystic, the inadequacy of the senses to give us insights that lie on a different level, and the capacity of the human spirit through this kind of insight to give assurance without logical reasoning. The mystic may or may not be familiar with the distinction made famous by William James between *knowledge about* and *knowledge of acquaintance*,[1] but it is the second of these that most concerns him. What he has seen and heard, touched and tasted with the eyes of the soul seems to him not only the most precious but the most dependable kind of knowledge. He may use the language of the senses or of reason to describe his experience after he has had it, but the experience itself does not center in these channels and is often said to be ineffable.

But what does the mystic reach out toward and receive assurance from in these blessed moments of spiritual or intuitive insight? In the order of existence, this is certainly the first consideration, though I am mentioning it third in order to begin with the human scene. It is primary to the mystic's vision and to much else, for without it there would be no mystical experience and no world.

This basic presupposition is of the existence of an Absolute, or a Ground of being, or the Ultimate Reality, or the Universal Self, or the One, which is above and beyond the visible world and on which all else depends. The Christian or Jewish mystic will speak of the One as God, the Islamic as Allah, the Hindu as Brahman, and there are other designations in other faiths and philosophies. But whatever the designation, every form of mysticism shares some such belief, even in those forms of Buddhism which claim to be atheistic, and as a result a sense of the holy and the sacred is a universal aspect of true mystical experience.

When the mystic's presuppositions as to human knowledge are placed in conjunction with the nature of ultimate reality, the result is belief that seems to require no argument. It is not "blind faith," for experience validates conviction. But neither is it "proof," as if one were to write Q.E.D. at the end of a proposition. The mystic feels that since one can know God by acquaintance, no argument is needed; and if one does not have this acquaintance by way of one's own experience no argument is useful.

A fourth presupposition which binds together the other three thus far mentioned is the capacity of the human spirit to come into union or communion with the One, or the Absolute, or with God. This is possible because of a receptivity or openness to divinity within the human spirit, whether it be termed Atman with the assertion that "That art thou," or in more familiar Christian terms, the Holy Spirit, "God present with us for guidance, for comfort, and for strength." [2] The union may consist of a brief, ecstatic sense of loss of one's own identity in the divine, which as previously indicated has often, but erroneously, been regarded as the only real type of mystical experience. It may mean also a sense of communion with "the Beyond that is within," for the most part quite steady and serene but with greater vividness at some times than others, and therefore with a greater sense of the immediacy of the divine Presence.

Two other presuppositions are almost always present in mystical experience, though they do not belong to its universal core as fully as those which have been stated. One of these is paradox. This is illustrated by the presence of God within the human soul, the Infinite within the finite, but it is so basic to any view of incarnation that it may not be recognized as paradoxical. There is a more questionable paradox in the affirmation that the individual does, and does not, lose his own identity in union with the divine. W.T. Stace in his comprehensive *Mysticism and Philosophy* maintains that every genuine mystical experience is marked by its "paradoxicality." [3]

The last presupposition which I shall mention is characteristic of Christian mysticism and it is accented in various other types, but I doubt that it can be said to be universal. This is the emphasis on purity of heart and life, with human goodness vital both to the preparation for and the fruit of the soul's meeting with Ultimate Good. It is perfectly epitomized in "Blessed are the pure in heart, for they shall see God." Strictly speaking, this is a moral rather than a philosophical ground, yet to the extent that morality forms a part of one's total world view, it is highly relevant. It is basic to the purgation which stands at the base of the mystical ladder, and it prompts the "self-naughting" which sometimes runs into asceticism but at its best means the purging of self-centeredness through the love of God and fellowman.

To anticipate the question of mysticism's objectivity, how valid are these presuppositions? They are in agreement with many aspects of religious faith not ordinarily termed mystical. The possibility of knowledge by insight or intuition has sound psychological standing. The modern philosophical tendency known as existentialism stresses personal existence and the human situation, including the very great importance of feeling, rather than logical deduction as a guide to truth. Whether or not anything is said about God in these fields, there are common epistemological presuppositions.

Yet to much of our secular, this-worldly, science-oriented society, the mystical experience is bound to seem like self-delusion or fantasy. Part of this judgment is based on a misunderstanding of what mysticism is, and an identification of it with the occult, with clairvoyance, with astrology and superstition. (If this book does no more than to clear up this misconstruction, it will have served a useful purpose!) Part of the adverse judgment against mysticism is more soundly based on the fact that some mystics have had psychotic tendencies. In general, however, the objection is that everything the individual thinks to be union or communion with the divine is the projection of the human ego.

One is, of course, entitled to this adverse opinion if he feels he must hold it. Yet if it is facts we seek, there is the undeniable fact that millions of people in many cultures and faiths throughout the world's history have accepted the mystic's presuppositions, though often without reflectively analyzing them, have had in some form a mystical experience, and have received from it a greater joy, peace, and personal stability than would have otherwise been possible. The mystic himself, even though he may not wish to argue, is willing to let the truth of his assumptions be tested by their fruits.

## 2. The Nature of the One

When we ask what is the One, or the Absolute, or the Universal Self with whom—or with which—the mystic feels himself united, the answers differ. There are differences within each major religion, and they appear in spite of similarities as one religion or culture is contrasted with another. I have not found the general nature of these differences more succinctly stated than by Stace in the book mentioned above:

> The Christian mystic usually says that what he experiences is "union with God." The Hindu mystic says that his experience is one in which his individual self is identical with Brahman or the Universal Self. The Christian says that his experience supports theism and is not an experience of actual identity with God, and he understands "union" as not involving identity but some other relation such as resemblance.

> The Hindu insists on identity, and says that his experience establishes what writers on mysticism usually call "pantheism"—though Hindus usually do not use that Western word. The Buddhist mystic—at least according to some versions of Buddhism—does not speak of God or Brahman or a Universal Self, but interprets his experience in terms which do not include the concept of a Supreme Being at all.[4]

Stace distinguishes between what he calls "extrovertive" and "introvertive" mysticism. The former is defined as that in which the mystic finds the One within the multiplicity of the things of nature. In the introvertive type there is an undifferentiated unity between the human self and that which, for lack of any distinguishing attributes, may even be termed the Void though it is also the Self. This latter type, which we have already encountered as the *via negativa,* is arrived at by the suppression of all sensations, sensory images, or rational thoughts, save perhaps one such as breathing or the repetition of a word or syllable as a means of shutting out all other elements of consciousness. This is clearly recognizable in Yoga, though it has its parallels elsewhere. When the mystic reaches this stage of undifferentiated unity within himself he also feels a complete sense of identification with the Universal Self.

But what of pantheism within these systems? The charge is often made that mysticism is by nature pantheistic, and therefore not authentically Christian. This is at best a half-truth, but there are forms of mysticism which give rise to this charge.

There is more than one type of extrovertive mysticism. Even if the term is limited to what is usually termed nature-mysticism, the finding of God with particular vividness within the realm of nature, it may or may not be pantheistic. If the natural order as a whole is identified with the One or the All, this is cosmic pantheism. However, in the Western world what is emphasized is more often a vivid sense of the divine immanence in all things rather than their identity with God. Note, for example, the "Canticle to the Sun" of St. Francis, which appears in many church hymnals with the title drawn from its opening words, "All creatures of our God and King." Or these familiar lines by William Wordsworth:

> And I have felt
> A presence that disturbs me with the joy
> Of elevated thoughts; a sense sublime

> Of something far more deeply interfused,
> Whose dwelling is the light of setting suns,
> And the round ocean and the living air,
> And the blue sky, and in the mind of man:
> A motion and a spirit, that impels
> All thinking things, all objects of all thought,
> And rolls through all things.[5]

In these lines, the Presence is felt to be "in the mind of man" and in "all thinking things, all objects of all thought." Yet even here there is no assertion of their full identity with the Presence. The extrovertive type of mysticism seldom denies that within the One or the All there is multiplicity, and thus it leaves room for at least the subordinate and temporal reality of both individual objects and individual persons.

The introvertive or subjective type of mysticism, which centers in distrust of all sensuous images and reflections upon them, is far more likely to be pantheistic, and its pantheism is of a different order from what this term ordinarily connotes. It may or may not affirm that the entire world of nature is *maya,* or illusion, but when it does, this is acosmic pantheism. In any case it presupposes the attainability of a state of complete identity of the human soul with the Over-Soul, or the One, in which all multiplicity disappears. Whatever its outlook on the world as a whole, it is pantheistic at this point. Its assumptions are expressed perfectly in one of the earliest pieces of mystical writing ever penned, the Hindu Mandukya Upanishad. In it the mystical consciousness is said to be "beyond the senses, beyond the understanding, beyond all expression. . . . It is the pure unitary consciousness, wherein awareness of the world and of multiplicity is completely obliterated. It is ineffable peace. It is the Supreme Good. It is One without a second. It is the Self." [6]

These words were written between three thousand and twenty-five hundred years ago. Yet they have a strangely modern sound, for it is this "ineffable peace" through the blotting out of normal sensations and intellectual processes, whether through imitation of some of the Oriental religions or through drugs, that has recently become very popular in our time.

Christian mysticism has seldom adopted a thoroughgoing pantheism. It is too foreign to the biblical and ecclesiastical outlook. Spinoza's *deus sive natura* which called for the viewing of all nature with religious reverence has seemed to go too far toward the equating of divinity with the natural order, and to founder, as any pantheism must, on the problem of evil. The Hegelian Absolute leans toward pantheism but does not quite cross the border, and has lost most of the standing it had in philosophical circles in the early part of this century. However, in various Christian writings of all periods there has cropped out a semi-pantheistic implication. This has appeared in both the extrovertive and introvertive types of mystical writing, with sometimes both types from the same author. This is true of Meister Eckhart, the most philosophically minded of all classical mystics in the Western tradition. Loyal Christian though he felt himself to be, a good many passages in his writings may be interpreted pantheistically, and for this reason he was considered a heretic by the ecclesiastical leaders of his time.

The mainstream of Christian thought, mystical and otherwise, has conceived of God in personal terms, though not as the Universal Self of Hindu writing. God is the Creator, the righteous Judge, the Redeemer, the Lord of history, the Father of our Lord Jesus Christ. These mainstream designations in conjunction with the Christian doctrine of the incarnation have prevented any major place being given to a pantheistic identification of God with the world or with the human self. But they have not stood in the way of the belief that the living God is both beyond and within this world and, furthermore, is both beyond and within the human self.

This is theism with an emphasis on both the transcendence and the immanence of God. Whenever the otherness without the immanence of God has been stressed, the result is deism—an external deity entering the world only occasionally by interventions, usually viewed as miracles. Whenever the immanence of God has been stressed without his transcendence, Christian faith has veered toward pantheism, and this has often passed over into humanism or a kind of naturalism with a religious aura. This position is characteristic of secular thought which has not entirely lost its religious foundations, and it is widely current today.

The main philosophical undergirding of Christian mysticism through the centuries has been this theism of a transcendent and immanent God, though the mystics themselves have seldom used this terminology. It may be called pan*en*theism if one desires a still more technical term for it. It will be recalled that when Biship John A. T. Robinson a few years ago produced his widely read *Honest to God,* he stirred up a considerable sensation by protesting against belief in a God "out there" or "up there." Doubtless he was justified in placing emphasis on the divine immanence and disclaiming spatial metaphors as to where God is. But to the degree that he seemed to inveigh against the divine transcendence, and not simply against too literal imagery, he was on unstable ground, and has since indicated his own affiliation with panentheism.[7]

No other position than theism will meet the requirements of Christian faith as a whole, to say nothing of its mystical elements. Without it there may be good thoughts, or good works, or even a considerable service to humanity, but not Christian faith. Yet Christian faith early in its history acquired accretions from Greek thought, and one line of this influence had a major effect on Christian mysticism, especially with reference to the *via negativa.* This must now be surveyed if we are to understand its philosophical grounds.

### 3. Early Philosophical Sources

Christian mysticism in its philosophical underpinning begins with Plato. This is not to say that Plato was a mystic for, as we found it necessary to say about Jesus, he was so much more that to affix this label to him would accent too strongly one side of manifold interests and contributions. Yet Plato's basic view of the universe, and certain strongly mystical passages in his writings, became the source of the Neoplatonism which through Plotinus and later Augustine entered the mainstream of Christian mysticism.

In the post-Apostolic period of the early church the affinities between Platonic and Christian thought were already being noted. Justin Martyr in the second century calls Plato "a Christian before Christ." Clement of Alexandria in the third calls the gospel "perfected Platonism." Ambrose felt impelled in the fourth to write a treatise to refute the charge that Christ had borrowed from Plato, and Augustine said that he had found in the Platonists everything but the incarnation.

This affinity stems primarily from the Platonic theory of Ideas, or Forms, which are held to constitute the real world above the things of earth, while these are imperfect copies. The supreme Idea is the Good, and Plato does not hesitate to speak of the Good as God. The highest human goodness is likeness to God; the highest happiness is the vision of God. Virtue must be sought for the health and harmony of the soul, for goodness *is* harmony with the Good which is the Real. Yet the Good stands for more than virtue in the ordinary sense; it incorporates in perfect form the archetypes, or original patterns, not only of goodness but of truth and beauty.

It would take us too far afield to comment on all aspects of Plato's thought, which is familiar to all students of the history of philosophy. It was not Christian, but was easily grafted on to the Christian concept of God as the Highest Good and the Source of all goodness, truth, and beauty. It then becomes both the supreme duty and the supreme delight of the individual to free himself from the entanglements of the flesh as far as possible, and in the heavenly vision find blessedness.

It is characteristic of Plato's mysticism, if it may be called that, to speak much more of vision than of union with God. But this is not vision in the ordinary sense of seeing, or thinking one sees, sensory objects. It is the kind of vision that sees truth or beauty with the eyes of the soul and through them sees the Good. We find this illustrated in two famous passages.

In the *Republic* is the allegory of the Cave, of which the central point is the shadowed nature of all earth-bound thinking, and the need to distinguish between illusion and reality. Prisoners chained all their lives in a cave, and able to see only the shadows of men passing by with the objects they carry, would think these shadows to be reality. The prisoners when brought to the light would at first be blinded, then see with a clarity impossible before, and they would not wish to return to the realm of shadows. Plato in exposition of the allegory speaks of the supernal light as "the intelligible realm," which is perceived only with difficulty but is the absolute form of the Good and the source of everything that is right and good in the realm of visible things.[8]

The passage on the ascent to absolute beauty, found in the *Symposium,* cannot be summarized and is too long to quote in full. Some excerpts will indicate its poetic imagery, though written in prose, and will suggest the Platonic vision of the Good and the human route of access to it.

> For he who has been taught in things of love so far, and who has learned to see the beautiful in order and succession, when he comes toward the end will suddenly perceive a world of beauty,— . . . not fair or foul, according to the point of view, or time, or place, but beauty absolute, apart; simple, and everlasting, without increase, decrease, or any change, imparted to the ever-growing changeful beauties of all other things; he who, impelled by love, uprising thence begins to see that beauty, nears the end.
>
> The time process, of being led to things of love, is this—to use earth's beauty as the stair up which he mounts to other beauty, going from one to all fair forms, and from fair forms to actions fair, to fair ideas, . . . until he comes to beauty absolute, to beauty's essence. . . .
>
> Do you not see that in this communion only, beholding beauty with the mind, he will be enabled to bring forth not images of beauty, but realities? For he has hold of a reality; he brings forth and educates true virtue; to become the friend of God and be immortal, if a mortal may. Would that be an ignoble life?[11]

While Plato identifies the Good with God, it is not God as a personal being that is the object of the quest for the ultimate in beauty, truth, and goodness. He seems in the *Timaeus* to have a personal God who as the Demiurge fashions the world out of chaos, but in much of his writing God is the supreme Goodness rather than a supremely good Being. This ambiguity was to have great influence in later developments.

It is in Plotinus (A.D. 205-270) that Neoplatonism comes to its fullest fruition, and no writing outside the Bible has been more determinative of the direction which the mysticism of the West was to take. He also influenced the East through the Sufis in Islamic mysticism. He was not a Christian but a Roman philosopher, affiliated with no religious creed or institution, but a deeply religious person, which is a significant evidence that mysticism can exist without a religious label. His early life was spent at Alexandria, a meeting-place of Eastern and Western currents of thought, but the last twenty-five years of his life were spent at Rome as a teacher of philosophy. His numerous writings were preserved by his pupil and biographer Porphyry as the Enneads or "nines," since they were arranged in six sections of nine books each. They contain many profound and beautiful passages.

The philosophy of Plotinus is not easy to grasp or to summarize. "To understand it at all one must put aside all ideas of time and space, of before and after, of here and now, of this and that, as we are conscious of them in the phenomenal world." [10] Yet despite the fact that our ordinary thinking is geared to a sense-bound world, I must try to state the main points of this paradoxical system.

Plotinus has a Trinity—a threefold Godhead—which is not the Christian Trinity though it has some points of contact with it. These are three forms of the Ultimate and the Real, the second emanating from the first and the third from the second, not identical and still not separate. If we speak of them as higher or lower we must avoid thinking of layers or levels, yet there are degrees of ultimacy in them. There are differences in their functions in relation to the world and ourselves, yet these differences within identity are not primarily functional but ontological. They are not three gods, but divinity in three basic modes.

The highest of these is what Plotinus calls the One, or the Source. This is not a personal Being with distinguishable attributes, but the Source of all being, that from which all else emanates. Says Plotinus, "This can be no thing among other things, but must be prior to all things." [11] The One is "fount of all that is best"; "great beyond anything great"; "infinite in fathomless depths of power"; "good in the unique mode of being the Good above all that is good"; "the fountain and principle of beauty." [12] It is beyond the range of human thought, for it is "a nobler Principle than anything we know as being, fuller and greater; above reason, mind and feeling." [13] Those familiar with the thought of the late Paul Tillich will detect here something much like his "Being-itself" that is not "a being" in the usual sense; rather, it is the "Ground of being" or "the Unconditioned."

The second element in the triad of Plotinus is directly traceable to Plato. It is *Nous,* or Mind, or "the intelligible realm," the sphere of eternal thought-forms or ideas or organizing principles. It includes the divine Mind and all forms and patterns of his thought. In it there is an identity of the Knower and the known. Furthermore, it knows no past or future, for in this noumenal world all things coexist in an Eternal Now.

It will be observed that the realm of *Nous,* though it is the realm of thought-forms as in Plato, has an affinity with the Logos of Stoic thought and of the prologue of John's Gospel. It is the principle of order and meaning that pervades all things. It permeates the world of spirit and of values as well as of intellectual processes. Yet it is unlike the Christian Logos, for there is no incarnation in a particular historical figure. Again the principle of emanation is in the foreground. *Nous* emanates from the One as light from the sun, or as heat from fire, not separate and yet not identical. Then from it proceeds the orderliness and intelligibility of the world. Our human minds, like the world of things, are an organic part of it, different and separate yet never severed from it.

The third element in the divine triad is the *Psyche*, or Soul, often called the Universal Soul or the Over-Soul. It is the principle of creative energy in all existence. Through it the eternal world of true being is linked with the world of time and space and imperfection. It makes the world of things and men into an organic, living whole, for in all things there is an indwelling life. It is eternal, and goes forth continuously to generate the world. In modern counterparts, this reminds one of the *élan vital* of Bergson or the "teleological creative advance" of Whitehead, though it is based not on any theory of evolution but on the emergence of all things from the Universal Soul. From it comes the soul of man, marred by imperfections but still belonging in its inmost nature to the world of *Nous*, and eternal. The body owes its origin to the soul, and not the soul to the body. Matter has no reality of its own and is the source of evil, though it is not wholly evil and the beauty of nature shows traces of the divine.

It has been necessary to summarize these main features of the thought of Plotinus to try to make clear the grounds of his mysticism and the reasons for his subsequent influence. The key to it is the One whose presence is felt on earth through his (or its?) Mind and Soul, to which human minds and souls owe their existence and in which they participate. There is difference, but also identity, between the human mind and soul and the divine. Because of this identity the true seeker after God becomes what he seeks; the seer becomes the Seen. Plotinus affirms this in a simple but striking analogy, "He belongs to God and is one with him, like two concentric circles; they are one when they coincide; and two only when they are separated."[14]

On this identity hinges the reality, the ecstasy and the ineffability of the mystic's vision. At this point I had better let Plotinus speak for himself in words which stand at the end of the *Enneads:*

> Since in the vision there were not two things, but seer and seen were one, . . . if a man could preserve the memory of what he was when he was mingled with the Divine, he would have in himself an image of Him. For he was then one with Him, and retained no difference, either in relation to himself or to others. Nothing stirred within him, neither anger nor concupiscence, nor even reason or spiritual perception or his own personality, if we may say so. Caught up in an ecstasy, tranquil and God-possessed, he enjoyed an imperturbable calm; shut up in his proper essence he inclined not to either side, he turned not even to himself; he was in a state of perfect stability; he had become stability itself. . . .
>
> If then a man sees himself become one with the One, he has in himself a likeness of the One, and if he passes out of himself, as an image to its archetype, he has reached the end of his journey. And when he comes down from his vision, he can again awaken the virtue that is in him, and seeing himself fitly adorned in every part he can again mount upward through virtue to Spirit, and through wisdom to the One itself. Such is the life of gods and of godlike and blessed men; a liberation from all earthly bonds, a life that takes no pleasure in earthly things, a flight of the alone to the Alone.[15]

These words, especially the last ones, have been quoted many times during the past seventeen centuries. In them we find a witness not only to the blessedness of the mystic's vision of God and its fruitfulness for personal living, but unfortunately to a less wholesome note. To withdraw from all earthly entanglements and to seek after "a life that takes no pleasure in earthly things" is not the good life as Jesus understood it. It has never been and ought never to become the dominant note in Christian mysticism.

For the present I shall bypass the Neoplatonism found in Augustine, for he was essentially a theologian rather than philosopher, and shall conclude this survey of early philosophical sources with a look at the pseudo-Dionysius, whom we shall call simply Dionysius. Despite his claim to be Dionysius the Areopagite of Acts 17:34 and his addressing Timothy in his writing to make the claim seem more plausible, there is a general consensus that he was a Syrian Christian of the late fifth or early sixth century. His work gained credence for centuries as being of apostolic origin, but must now stand on its own merits.

Dionysius was a Neoplatonist in the general tradition of Plotinus, and the blend of this stream with his Christian faith gave rise to some new emphases. He wrote four treatises and some letters which have been preserved, and two of these, his *Mystical Theology* and *The Divine Names* had considerable influence on Western mysticism. The other two, the *Celestial Hierarchy* and the *Ecclesiastical Hierarchy,* show both an advanced institutional development in the church beyond that of the first century and the influence of Plotinus' thought of the emergence of lower forms from the higher, with the light of the higher still illumining them. They need not concern us in this study.

While Dionysius is now thought of primarily as being in the vanguard of Christian mysticism of the *via negativa* type, he can also be credited with raising a question which has of late swung into much prominence in philosophical discussion. This is the question of the nature and the legitimacy of religious language.

Let us begin with *The Divine Names.* Its primary emphasis is the complete impossibility of saying what God is. This was not wholly new, for it had long been affirmed in Indian philosophy and was foreshadowed in Plotinus' concept of the One. In the Upanishads God is "not this, not that." But Dionysius has a long list of more than fifty terms as to what God is not!

> We maintain that He is neither soul nor intellect; nor has He imagination, opinion, reason, or understanding; nor can he be expressed or conceived, since He is neither number nor order; nor greatness nor smallness; nor equality nor inequality, . . . neither has He power, nor is power, nor is light; neither does He live, nor is He life; neither is He essence, nor eternity, nor time.

The negations go on and on, as if the author were about to say that there is no God at all. But not so. The list ends with these important words:

> Although we may affirm or deny the things below Him, we can neither affirm nor deny Him, inasmuch as the all-perfect and unique Cause of all things transcends all affirmation, and the simple pre-eminence of His absolute nature is outside of every negation—free from every limitation and beyond them all.[16]

In short, God is so transcendent that he is beyond all human knowledge. But from this sentence it becomes evident that Dionysius believes we do at least know that God is "the all-perfect and unique Cause of all things."

This gives him a way out for terms such as wisdom, power, goodness, love, which as a Christian one must use about God. Such terms, he says, are not descriptions standing for the known attributes of God, but symbols by which the human mind tries to apprehend the utterly transcendent being of God. The symbols arise from what the Cause has produced within the world we know, and are legitimate if they are used with the recognition that these are "the metaphorical titles drawn from the world of sense and applied to the nature of God." He even grants that some of these "metaphorical titles" are much more appropriate than others.

> For is it not more true to affirm that God is Life and Goodness than that He is air or stone; and must we not deny to Him more emphatically the attributes of inebriation and wrath than the applications of human speech and thought?[17]

Not only is this symbolism of Dionysius an interesting development in itself, but we may note from it that such defenders of the symbolic nature of religious language as Rudolf Otto and Paul Tillich have a precedent in the long past.

To turn to the mysticism of Dionysius, he exerted an important influence at two points. He did not originate the *via negativa,* but he gave it a great forward thrust by describing the mystical consciousness at its most profound—or its most abstract—level. The philosophical and psychological undergirding which he gave it had great influence in later mystical writing. Furthermore, his concept of the absolute transcendence of God both to the world and to human knowledge is responsible for the term "the Divine Darkness" which appears repeatedly.

The Divine Darkness is a realm of silence as well as of dark. Yet in mystical experience at its climax, even this utter darkness is suffused with the brilliance of celestial light. Although Dionysius designates the short treatise which describes it as *Mystical Theology,* it is not theology in the usual sense which is thus imparted to the seeker. Rather, it is heavenly Truth which in the union with God breaks through with a joyous unveiling which

Dionysius calls "the superessential Radiance of the Divine Darkness."

If this does not seem very plausible to the scientifically oriented mind of the twentieth century, it is not surprising. Since I myself hold no brief for it, I had better let Dionysius speak for it.

> Supernal Triad, deity above all essence, knowledge and goodness; Guide of Christians to Divine Wisdom; direct our path to the ultimate summit of Thy mystical Lore, most incomprehensible, most luminous, and most exalted, where the pure, absolute, and immutable mysteries of theology are veiled in the dazzling obscurity of the secret Silence, outshining all brilliance with the intensity of their Darkness, and surcharging our blinded intellects with the utterly impalpable and invisible fairness of glories surpassing all beauty.
>
> Let this be my prayer; but do thou, dear Timothy, in the diligent exercise of mystical contemplation, leave behind the senses and the operations of the intellect, and all things sensible and intellectual, and all things in the world of being and non-being, that thou mayest arise, by unknowing, towards the union, as far as is attainable, with Him who transcends all being and all knowledge. For by the unceasing and absolute renunciation of thyself and of all things, thou mayest be borne on high, through pure and entire self-abnegation, into the superessential Radiance of the Divine Darkness.[18]

Questions immediately emerge. Is this realism or self-deception? Has Dionysius carried the mystic's union with the Divine, not only beyond the bounds of the five senses as he advocates, but beyond sound sense and credibility? To this inquiry we must now turn.

## 4. The Objectivity of the Mystical Experience

In considering whether the mystic actually meets or merges with Ultimate Reality, a number of considerations must be kept in mind. The first of these is whether the experience *as experience,* apart from the question of its interpretation, has been correctly reported. If not, we need go no further.

The second is the relation between value and validity. Some things have value which have no objective reference. A person may feel immensely buoyed up by the belief that he has a loyal friend or spouse, or abundant financial resources, or a long time yet to live, and none of these assumptions may be true. The commonest charge against religion as a whole is that it is based on a gigantic illusion. But do we live in a total realm of illusion in which our most precious grounds of assurance have no foundations? Few would say so. Then how do we distinguish reality from illusion?

A third factor, very important to the theme we are considering, is the distinction between various types of mysticism. If the negative way is the only type, then this narrows considerably the frame of discussion. Yet we have noted that Rufus M. Jones during a lifetime of studies in this field regarded the union with an "abstract Infinite" as being by no means the only or the most fruitful type of mystical experience. Dean William R. Inge, also a highly respected authority, does not hesitate to say, "I regard the *via negativa* in metaphysics, religion, and ethics as the great accident of Christian Mysticism," though he qualifies this statement by saying that he does not think the negative road is pure error.[19] If there is more than one kind of mysticism, we must ask whether some types have objective reality while others do not.

Finally, underlying all these questions is the relation of psychological to ontological reality. Unfortunately, we have to use the word "real" for both. But as was suggested at the end of our first chapter, the two fields have different purposes and there is no necessary conflict between them.

To begin with the first question, we can eliminate from classical mysticism any attempt at conscious deception. The mystics took the experience too seriously for that. I am not sure but that in some contemporary forms of mysticism, so-called, which are induced by drugs or by a faddist imitation of Oriental practices, there may be some reporting which tells a dramatic story for effect. There is no evidence of this among the mystics whose experience we shall examine in Part Two of this book.

Even so, it could be that the mystic reports his experience incorrectly. The mystic frequently says that his ecstatic experience is indescribable; then he proceeds to describe it. Does he report it accurately?

The answer to this question lies in the fact that in *any* experience, whether sensory, rational, emotional, or mystical, there is no raw experience that does not pass through the crucible of the mind's interpretation. As in the old analogy of the five blind men and the elephant, what one sees, feels, or thinks is colored by the subject's prior experience. In the field of sense experience, a mirage or the apparently converging lines of a railroad track or the bent stick in a pool of water can be tested out by the consensus of evidence from other angles and the general agreement of observers. In the matter of mystical experience, the problem is complicated by the fact that while there is a large consensus among those who have had it, many people have never had it. Yet the fact that it is relatively rare ought not to cancel out the witness of those to whom it is a living fact.

To move to the question of value and validity, the two are not identical and it is obviously possible to find contentment and happiness temporarily in illusions taken for realities. The pragmatic argument alone will not prove the mystic's assumptions to be objectively grounded. Yet there is a connection, for life as a whole is lived on the basis of unproved assumptions as to the dependability of the natural order and of human relations. When the fruits of mystical experience cohere with a healthy outlook on the totality of human existence, there is strong ground for believing that the subject is in touch with reality. St. Teresa of Avila put this vividly in these words:

> If one were to tell me that a person with whom I had just conversed, and whom I knew well, was not that person, but that I was deluding myself, and that they knew it, I should certainly trust them rather than my own eyes. But if that person left with me certain jewels—and if, possessing none previously, I held the jewels in my hand as pledges of a great love—and if I were now rich, instead of poor as before . . .

then she would have to believe. The jewels to which she refers are tenderness, joy, humility, peace, insight.[20]

We come now to the distinctions between types of mysticism. These need to be examined in the light of the coherence of all factors. Not the least of these is coherence with one's basic theological or philosophical outlook. A point of view which denies that anything exists except the physical world and such human mentality as is derived from and dependent on it will find no place for Transcendent Reality, whether in mysticism or elsewhere. The pantheist who identifies the Divine with the All will ordinarily find no problem in the belief that the mystic's experience of union with God is a special case of such identity.

Even if the pantheism is of the type which finds the divine immanence in all things but without transcendence, nature-mysticism is a natural product of this point of view.

The panentheist or personalist must speak more guardedly. He believes that communion with God is entirely possible—a normative and true experience consistent both with biblical faith and a personal God of creativity, wisdom, goodness, and love. Believing God to be immanent in the world of things and persons as well as transcendent to them, he finds an openness to divinity within the human spirit. If he stands within the Christian tradition, he believes in the Holy Spirit as giving special guidance and strengthening when sought or allowed to speak. He does not deny that even in the more extreme forms of mystical experience, God is present to the individual. What he does feel constrained to deny is that the mystic's interpretation of his union with God as loss of his own identity is a true interpretation. However much one may lose the awareness of his own self-consciousness, man remains man and God is God.

What then of the psychological aspects of this experience? There is no need to deny that the kind of experience one has, whether mystical or otherwise, depends largely on temperament, past experience, social conditioning, and the immediate stimulus. There is nothing abnormal about a sense of divine companionship in communion with God; it is so normal to serious religious experience that many refuse to call it mystical.

When mysticism is identified with a loss of self-awareness in the ecstatic rapture of what is believed to be a passing but indescribably blessed union with God, what occurs may be a form of trance. Evelyn Underhill in her classic and comprehensive *Mysticism* does not hesitate to call it trance in its physical expressions and mono-ideism in its psychological nature.[21] Since trances are not everyday occurrences, this makes it an abnormal experience. But this does not disqualify it from being a genuine experience of God. In ordinary speech "entrancing" is not a term of disparagement—why should it be in mystical language? The abnormal can be either subnormal or supernormal, the distinction to be judged by the fruits and the total relationship to life.

So, I do not disparage the mystic's rapture, even though it come to him in ways that I believe I should be temperamentally unable to experience. Though I believe the way of affirmation and communion to be normally the better route than that of negation and union, we have noted that it is difficult to draw a sharp line between them. What matters most is that the individual open his life to God and from this openness find richer and more fruitful living.

# PART TWO

# IV

# Early and Medieval Mysticism

With this chapter we begin a new type of procedure. The aim of the remainder of the book will not be primarily to describe and evaluate the various types of mysticism, though this will not be left behind, but rather to induce a living, personal acquaintance with certain of the great mystics. Because of an enduring message, their devotional writings have left a stamp on Western history. Some of them such as St. Augustine and St. Francis have names familiar to everybody, though it cannot be assumed that their devotional insights are equally familiar. Others are less well known. Yet known or unknown, they have been selected for presentation because they have something vital to say to the world of today.

The late Willard L. Sperry in his delightful *Strangers and Pilgrims*[1] uses an analogy which is worth passing on. The theological works coming out of the past are like rocks in the earth's surface, stratified according to the successive ages in which they were laid down. The classics of Christian devotion, on the other hand, are the primal unstratified stuff of Christian living. They reflect the aspirations, the achievements and the abundant blessings of Christian experience in every age. For this reason they are timeless.

## 1. St. Augustine

We begin with Augustine, not primarily because he was the major theological giant of Western Christendom whose thought is still influential, but because his mystical writing is so illuminating and poignant. It does not appear all in one place and it has to be sorted out from various sources, of which the *Confessions* is the principal one. Yet it is unmistakably present, not in the most extreme forms of union with God, but in numerous passages which glow with a deep spiritual insight.

It is often said that mystical experience does not combine well, if at all, with the life of the intellect, or with administrative duties, or with ecclesiastical authority, or with the practical affairs of everyday life. Augustine is the living refutation of all these assumptions. His massive intellectual achievements, both directly through his own theological works and indirectly through Catholic thought in Thomas Aquinas and Reformation thought in Luther, have influenced the theology of the Western Church more than any other person except Paul. As the Bishop of Hippo he wielded much power and engaged in history-making contests with Pelagius and with the Donatists. He was firmly dogmatic in his theology and would countenance no irregularities. And as an ecclesiastical statesman who was also warm-hearted in relation to individuals, "he was full of business, a bishop devoted to his flock, a popular preacher, a letter-writer ever ready to answer, even at great length, the questions put to him." [2]

All these activities and achievements we must leave aside in this survey and center on his personal Christian experience. Yet who knows but that without this aspect of Augustine's inner life, his public contributions would have left far less of a legacy to history?

The outward facts of his life are well known but may be briefly traced. He was born at Tagaste, one of the smaller cities of North Africa, in 354. His father, Patricius, not a Christian, died when Augustine was in his teens and does not figure prominently in the story. His mother, Monica, does. She was a devout Christian who never ceased to yearn and pray for the conversion of her only son until this occurred when he was thirty-two.

His parents, aware of the talents of the young Augustine, saw to it that he was prepared for the profession of teacher of rhetoric. His studies and later his teaching took him by stages from Tagaste to Carthage and then to Italy, first to Rome and then to Milan. At nineteen, in reading Cicero's *Hortensius,* he was quickened to a quest for religious truth. For a time he was attracted to the Manichaean dualistic philosophy which viewed evil as caused by a force of darkness contending eternally with the good in the universe and in the soul of man. Dissatisfied with this, he was plunged into a period of skepticism, from which he was considerably lifted by turning to Neoplatonism, and he absorbed elements of the thought of Plotinus which never left him. We shall presently note its effects emerging in his mysticism.

During the course of these intellectual struggles as a young man trying to find himself he felt powerfully the force of sexual temptation, and yielded to it. In retrospect, as Augustine in the *Confessions* tells of this experience, it sounds like unrestrained lechery, but is probably overstated. He took an unnamed mistress who was faithful to him for many years and bore him a son whom he named Adeodatus, "the gift of God." This does not sound like sheer profligacy. At Monica's insistence he put her away in order to enter into a legal marriage which never took place. A little later his conversion and subsequent ordination to the priesthood put an end to thoughts of marriage, and as far as the record indicates, of sex as well.

Augustine was converted in the late summer of 386 and baptized at the Easter season of the next year. Before his conversion Monica had joined him in Milan, and on their way back to North Africa in 388 she died at the port of Ostia. After several years of seclusion in which he lived at first according to monastic rules and then entered the priesthood he was made Bishop of Hippo. He held this office until his death in 430, just as Hippo was being beseiged by the Vandals. It was the imminent collapse of Rome as a great power which prompted another lasting work, *The City of God,* in which the church is viewed as able to withstand any political dissolution. The *Confessions,* written in 397, a year or two after he became bishop, is one of the world's greatest spiritual autobiographies. In it we see his struggle not only with sex but with pride, self-will, and personal ambition, jointly designated as concupiscence. Delivery from it by God's grace was a major note in his theology.

Whatever may be thought of Augustine's early sexual misadventures, there were some mitigating circumstances. For one thing, monogamous concubinage was generally accepted at the time. For another, they did not stand in the way of a pure and deep devotion to his mother, who though a Christian appears to have been a rather dominating person who tried to shape her son's life to her wishes. Had Augustine been as bad a sinner as he portrays himself, he would hardly have engaged in such a serious and continuous search for a true understanding of life.

Furthermore, he was an outgoing person with a deep capacity for response to the best in other persons, whether one of high estate like Bishop Ambrose or the friends in whom he found deep enrichment for his soul. It was his grief over the early death of one of these friends that prompted him to place in the *Confessions* a description of friendship which is perhaps unexcelled in all literature:

> To talk and jest together, to do kind offices by turns; to read together honeyed books; to play the fool or be earnest together; to dissent at times without discontent, as a man might with his own self; and even with the seldomness of these dissentings, to season our more frequent consentings; sometimes to teach, and sometimes to learn; long for the absent with impatience; and welcome the coming with joy. These and the like expressions, proceeding out of the hearts of those that loved and were loved again, by the countenance, the tongue, the eyes, and a thousand pleasing gestures, were so much fuel to melt our souls together, and out of many make but one.[3]

Only an unusually warm-hearted individual in his personal relations could have written such a passage.

Granting these facts, it still can scarcely be doubted that Augustine's sexual struggle was a real one from the place it occupies in his conversion. There we see a double set of powerful forces in conjunction: a consciousness of guilt—in more traditional language a conviction of sin, and the coming into focus of a long stream of Christian influences which for years had been tugging at his mind and soul, half-accepted and half-rejected. As with Paul, the conversion happened suddenly but with years of preparation back of it.

The story is a familiar one, but perhaps we had better let Augustine tell the most crucial parts of it in his own words. He tells how in great agitation of spirit he one day sought out the little garden of the lodging where he lived with his friend Alypius, whose silent understanding comes through very clearly in the account.

> But when a deep consideration had from the secret bottom of my soul drawn together and heaped up all my misery in the sight of my heart; there arose a mighty storm, bringing a mighty shower of tears. . . . I cast myself down I know not how, under a certain fig-tree, giving full vent to my tears; and the floods of mine eyes gushed out, an *acceptable sacrifice to Thee.* And, not indeed in these words, yet to

> this purpose, spake I much unto Thee: *And Thou, O Lord, how long? how long, Lord, wilt Thou be angry, for ever? Remember not our former iniquities,* for I felt that I was held by them. I sent up these sorrowful words; How long? how long? "tomorrow, and tomorrow?" Why not now? why not is there this hour an end to my uncleanness?

At this moment he heard the voice of a child from a neighboring house saying, "Take up and read; take up and read." Thinking this might be the command of God, he picked up the New Testament from where he had been sitting earlier with Alypius. Let us return to his own words.

> I seized, opened, and in silence read that section, on which my eyes first fell: *Not in rioting and drunkenness, not in chambering and wantonness, not in strife and envying: but put ye on the Lord Jesus Christ, and make not provision for the flesh,* in concupiscence. No further would I read; nor needed I; for instantly at the end of this sentence, by a light as it were of serenity infused into my heart, all the darkness of doubt vanished away.[4]

The next step was to inform Monica of what had happened, at which she rejoiced greatly. The closing words of the chapter tell between the lines a good deal about both Augustine and his mother. "For thou convertedst me unto Thyself, so that I sought neither wife, nor any hope of this world. . . . And Thou didst convert her mourning into joy, much more plentiful than she had desired, and in a much more precious and purer way than she erst required, by having grandchildren of my body." [5]

I have included this account of Augustine's conversion for the light it throws on him as a person, not as evidence of his mysticism, though the latter can scarcely be understood apart from the man he was—a person of massive intellect and unremitting quest, frustrated in self-mastery until he found rest in God. He epitomizes in his experience the most familiar of all his words, from the first page of the *Confessions,* "Thou madest us for Thyself, and our heart is restless, until it repose in Thee." [6] Yet the conversion experience itself hardly qualifies as mystical. It is definitely less so than Paul's, for the voice that Augustine heard was apparently that of a flesh-and-blood child in a nearby house, and his response to the words of Scripture fits directly his state of mind. This is certainly not to deny the presence of God in the event, but it is not the usual mystical way of thinking of such Presence.

However, there are other passages in the *Confessions* which are both autobiographical and mystical. The earliest of these, which occurred before his conversion but after he had become acquainted with Neoplatonism, show clearly the influence of Plotinus. He speaks of finding in "certain books of the Platonists" a note very similar to the opening words of John's Gospel and numerous other passages of Scripture. But not wholly, and the difference at a vital point was great. "But that *the Word was made flesh, and dwelt among us,* I read not there." [7] Yet this did not lead him to reject them; God might be speaking through them. "And I had come to Thee from among the Gentiles; and I set my mind upon the gold which Thou willedst Thy people to take from Egypt, seeing Thine it was, wheresoever it were." [8] This reference to the gold from Egypt doubtless refers to Plotinus, though he is not mentioned by name. Then this passage on the Light Unchangeable directly follows:

> And being thence admonished to return to myself, I entered even into my inward self, Thou being my Guide: and able I was, for Thou wert become my Helper. And I entered and beheld with the eye of my soul, (such as it was,) above the same eye of my soul, above my mind, the Light Unchangeable. Not this ordinary light, which all flesh may look upon, nor as it were a greater of the same kind, as though the brightness of this should be manifold brighter, and with its greatness take up all space. Not such was this light, but other, yea, far other from all these. Nor was it above my soul, as oil is above water, nor yet as heaven above earth: but above to my soul, because It made me; and I below It, because I was made by It. He that knows the Truth, knows what that Light is; and he that knows It, knows eternity. Love knoweth it. O Truth Who art Eternity! and Love Who art Truth! and Eternity Who art Love! Thou art my God, to Thee do I sigh night and day. . . . And Thou didst beat back the weakness of my sight, streaming forth Thy beams of light upon me most strongly, and I trembled with love and awe.[9]

This blend of Platonism with Christian insight and, in retrospect, deep devotion provides the intellectual and spiritual groundwork for another experience, unmistakably mystical, which is described a few pages further on in the same chapter. It is unclear whether this refers to another experience of divine immediacy, or to the same one described from the angle of ascent from the ordinary channels of sense and reason to the Ultimate Reality which he calls the Unchangeable.

> Step by step was I led upwards, from bodies to the soul which perceives by means of the bodily senses; and thence to the soul's inward faculty to which the bodily senses report external things, which is the limit of the intelligence of animals; and thence again to the reasoning faculty, to whose judgement is referred the knowledge received by the bodily senses. And when this power also within me found itself changeable, it lifted itself up to its own intelligence, and withdrew its thoughts from experience, abstracting itself from the contradictory throng of sense images, that it might find what that light was wherein it was bathed when it cried out that beyond all doubt the unchangeable is to be preferred to the changeable; whence also it knew That Unchangeable: and thus with the flash of one trembling glance it arrived at THAT WHICH IS.[10]

Such words as these could have been written by Plotinus. They are in keeping with Augustine's affirmation elsewhere that "that truly is, which remains unchangeably."[11] Yet Augustine found no great difficulty in blending this note of Platonic realism with the Hebraic I AM THAT I AM. Commenting on the latter in another treatise, *Concerning the Nature of the Good,* he states, "For He truly Is, because He is unchangeable; for all change causes that which was, not to Be. He then truly Is, who is unchangeable."[12] Thus the passage does not lack its divine reference even though God is not directly named in it.

However, the most distinctively mystical passage in the *Confessions* is that in which Augustine describes beautifully the moment of mystical communion which he experienced with his mother at the port of Ostia shortly before her death. Some lines from this were quoted in chapter one, but it needs to be seen in its fuller setting.

> And when our discourse was brought to that point, that the very highest delight of the earthly senses, in the very purest material light, was, in respect of the sweetness of that life, not only not worthy of comparison, but not even of mention; we raising up ourselves with a more glowing affection towards the "Self-same" [the unchanging God], did by degrees pass through all things bodily, even the very heaven, whence sun and moon and stars shine upon the earth; yea, we were soaring higher yet, by inward musing, and discourse, and admiring of Thy works; and we came to our own minds, and went beyond

them, that we might arrive at that region of never-failing plenty, where *Thou feedest Israel* for ever with the food of truth.[13]

Augustine injects some words about the eternity of Wisdom, and says they "returned to vocal expressions." Yet he continues in the same mystical mood:

We were saying then: If to any the tumult of the flesh were hushed, hushed the images of earth, and waters, and air, hushed also the poles of heaven, yea the very soul be hushed to herself, and by not thinking on self surmount self, hushed all dreams and imaginary revelations, every tongue and every sign, and whatsoever exists only in transition, since if any could hear, all these say, *We made not ourselves, but He made us that abideth for ever*—If then having uttered this, they too should be hushed, having roused only our ears to Him who made them, and He alone speak, not by them, but by Himself, that we may hear His Word, not through any tongue of flesh, nor angel's voice, nor sound of thunder, nor in the dark riddle of a similitude, but, might hear Whom in these things we love, might hear His Very, Self without these, (as we two now strained ourselves, and in swift thought touched on that Eternal Wisdom, which abideth over all;)—could this be continued on, and other visions of kind far unlike be withdrawn, and this one ravish, and absorb, and wrap up its beholder amid these inward joys, so that life might be forever like that one moment of understanding which now we sighed after; were not this, *Enter into thy Master's joy?* [14]

All the most typical notes of mystical experience are here—the transcendence of sense experience, the entrance into one's deepest self, the hushed silence, the certainty of the Divine Presence, the inexpressible joy. The upward passage through the things of earth to the blessedness of communion with the Eternal Wisdom is reminiscent of Plato's call "to use earth's beauty as the stair up which he mounts to other beauty . . . until he comes to beauty absolute, to beauty's essence." [15] Yet one feels that the mood here, even if touched with Platonism, is deeply Christian. It was shared by Monica who knew nothing of Platonism and is described by Augustine through a Christian perspective some nine years after the occurrence. Unless we are to limit the meaning of mysticism to the union of the human self with God in ontological identity, which Augustine nowhere affirms, it is one of the most authentically mystical passages in all literature.

It must be evident that Augustine's type of mysticism is both intellectual and devotional, with the two elements so closely blended that it is futile to try to separate them. He also had a remarkable gift of language in describing his thoughts and feelings. I must close this review of his thought by citing some passages which demonstrate these features, and which though not mystical except in a broad sense are deeply devotional.

To a degree unique among the mystics, Augustine combines an intellectual vision of spiritual things with a passionate love of God. Furthermore, in the following passage he has told us *how* he loves God.

> Not with doubting, but with assured consciousness, do I love Thee, Lord. . . . But what do I love, when I love Thee? not beauty of bodies, nor the fair harmony of time, nor the brightness of the light, so gladsome to our eyes, nor sweet melodies of varied songs, nor the fragrant smell of flowers, and ointments, and spices, not manna and honey, not limbs acceptable to embracements of flesh. None of these I love, when I love my God; and yet I love a kind of light, and melody, and fragrance, and meat, and embracement, when I love my God, the light, melody, fragrance, meat, embracement of my inner man; where there shineth unto my soul, what space cannot contain, and there soundeth, what time beareth not away, and there smelleth, what breathing disperseth not, and there tasteth, what eating diminisheth not, and there clingeth, what satiety divorceth not. This is it which I love, when I love my God.[16]

There is no mention here of what the love of God means in terms of love of one's fellowmen. From this angle the statement is incomplete. Yet seldom, if ever, has a finer statement been penned as to the difference between sensory enjoyment and true worship. It might well be taken to heart as a criterion for distinguishing between the sensory accompaniments of worship, so common in the churches of today, and that commitment of the self in worship which springs from the love of God.

It will be recalled that Augustine lived two centuries before the pseudo-Dionysius, who spoke of "the Divine Darkness" and who believed that no descriptive attributes could be affirmed of God. He might well have learned something more positive from Augustine, who found plenty to say of the nature of God, and in doing so proved himself a master of the language of paradox. Almost at the beginning of the *Confessions* we find these words:

> What art Thou, then, my God? What, but the Lord God? *For who is Lord but the Lord? or who is God save our God?* Most highest,

most good, most potent, most omnipotent; most merciful, yet most just; most hidden, yet most present; most beautiful, yet most strong; stable, yet incomprehensible; unchangeable, yet all-changing; never new, never old; all renewing, and *bringing age upon the proud, and they know it not;* ever working, ever at rest; still gathering, yet nothing lacking; supporting, filling, and over-spreading; creating, nourishing, and maturing; seeking, yet having all things. Thou lovest, without passion; art jealous, without anxiety; repentest, yet grievest not; art angry, yet serene; changest Thy works, Thy purpose unchanged; receivest again what Thou findest, yet never didst lose; never in need, yet rejoicing in gains; never covetous, yet exacting usury. Thou receivest over and above, that Thou mayest owe; and who hath aught that is not Thine? Thou payest debts, owing nothing; remittest debts, losing nothing. And what have I now said, my God, my life, my holy joy? or what saith any man when he speaks of Thee? Yet woe to him that speaketh not, since mute are even the most eloquent.[17]

Follow this passage through, and one finds here and there a term to question. Yet taken as a whole, it is a glorious affirmation of the God of Christian faith. The final sentence is a particularly poignant statement of the perennial truth that speak of God we must, though fitting speech eludes us.

One more citation must suffice, and I choose it because it brings together so vividly his early struggles and his mature faith, and in a sense gives the key to that which was to make him a foremost figure in history.

Too late loved I Thee, O thou Beauty of ancient days, yet ever new! too late I loved Thee! And behold, Thou wert within, and I abroad, and there I searched for Thee; deformed I, plunging amid those fair forms, which Thou hadst made. Thou wert with me, but I was not with Thee. Things held me far from Thee, which, unless they were in Thee, were not at all. Thou calledst, and shoutedst, and burstest, my deafness. Thou flashedst, shonest, and scatteredst my blindness. Thou breathedst odors, and *I drew in breath* and *pant for Thee.* I tasted, and *hunger and thirst.* Thou touchedst me, and I burned for Thy peace.[18]

Archaic though the language is, the message comes through. It is probably superfluous to say that it is one which the world needs greatly today. "Thou wert with me, but I was not with Thee." This sums up the human predicament, and the way of delivery from it.

Augustine left to posterity a doctrine of God and man, and of sin and grace, which I have not attempted to spell out. So also his doctrine of the church, and the ecclesiastical structure he so largely helped to fashion. But along with these he left a deeply devotional spirit that speaks today to the sensitive listener. Whatever conflicts there may appear to be between these variant streams of thought, they were reconciled in his own life with God.

## 2. St. Bernard

The work of Augustine stands just before the beginning of the medieval period. The limits of space require us to pass by Gregory the Great (ca. 540-604), a pope who did much to solidify the ecclesiastical structure, establish monasticism, and popularize the thought of Augustine, and who also left significant writing on the personal Christian life. Also John Scotus Erigena (810-877), who by his translation of the work of the pseudo-Dionysius from Greek to Latin did much to introduce this type of thought into the Western church. Bypassing also some less well-known figures, we come to St. Bernard, who stands near the climax of the medieval period.

Bernard of Clairvaux lived at the height of the twelfth-century Renaissance. It was a great century—not solely the century of the Crusades which have cast a dark shadow over it, but of the rise of important towns, the beginnings of Gothic architecture, the founding of the first universities, the beginnings of literature written in the language of the people, the recovery of Greek philosophy through Moslem contacts. Into this world came Bernard, who as a humble churchman was to wield a powerful influence, both as a dominant public figure in his own day and on the inner life of Christians for centuries. Even today, almost every church hymnal contains the words attributed to him:

> Jesus, thou joy of loving hearts!
> Thou fount of life! Thou light of men!
> From the best bliss that earth imparts,
> We turn unfilled to thee again.

These words epitomize the undergirding of his life, which can here be only briefly summarized. He was born into a noble family in France, his father being in military service and his mother an unusually devout and compassionate woman who engaged personally in much service to the sick and the poor. After the death of both parents he went at twenty-two into a small isolated Benedictine monastery at Citeaux. His ability soon becoming apparent, he was sent after three years with twelve other monks to found a new monastery at Clairvaux. There he remained as its abbot for the rest of his life, extending the outreach of the Church until sixty-eight daughter-monasteries had been formed, preaching eloquently over a wide territory as well as in the chapel at Clairvaux, serving as counselor to popes and kings, and meanwhile writing lasting treatises on the inner life. He was a poet of no small ability, and his hymns alone would have assured him a permanent place in Christian history.

Among his major public activities was his intervention in an eight-year struggle between two rival claimants which resulted in the seating of Gregory, then to be known as Innocent II, as the rightful pope. A former pupil of Bernard's later became Pope Eugenius III, in no small measure through his influence, and in the treatise *De Consideratione* he gives him bold and frank advice about the duties and responsibilities of his office.[19] He did not hesitate to counsel King Louis VII about both his private and his public life. The public activity for which he is most remembered is his extensive preaching in support of the Second Crusade, which rallied thousands to engage in it though as a churchman he did not do so personally. Its failure caused him deep unhappiness.

All this would be irrelevant in an account of Bernard as a devotional writer except that, as with Augustine, it shows that it is possible to combine a very active public life with a deeply devotional spirit. Unlike Augustine he was not an original theologian, his outlook being the orthodox one which caused him to oppose vigorously what he viewed as the heresy of Abelard. Yet he had a deep sense of the nature and fruits of the love of God, of the need of combining humility with charity, and of the primacy of Jesus, which have not always been found in either theological orthodoxy or ecclesiastical statemanship.

I shall begin a survey of Bernard's devotional writing with what he says of Jesus, for it is necessary at the outset to answer a charge often brought against him and other mystics who speak of "spiritual marriage." His major writing is found in a collection of eighty-six sermons on *The Song of Songs,* or *The Song of Solomon* as it is now more commonly designated. This Old Testament book is now regarded by biblical scholars as a collection of romantic wedding lyrics. Yet it was long regarded as an allegory foreshadowing the church as the Bride of Christ. It is so indicated in the headings of a King James version of the Bible which stands today on my bookshelves, and nobody in Bernard's time thought otherwise. Indeed, with references in the book of Revelation to "the Bride, the wife of the Lamb" (Revelation 21:9) and to "the Spirit and the Bride" (Revelation 22:17), it would have been strange if any other interpretation had been given.

With this background, Jesus Christ throughout the sermons of Bernard is the Bridegroom. He does not use the term "spiritual marriage" as freely as did some of the later mystics, but its imagery is there. Taking up the opening words of the *Song*, "Let him kiss me with the kisses of his mouth" (1:2), he describes the three stages of spiritual progression, the purgative, the illuminative, and the unitive, as the kiss of the Feet, the kiss of the Hand, and the kiss of the Mouth of Christ. The first involves penitence and pardon; it is the conversion stage. In the second the fruits of piety appear through grace, and good works are possible. In the third, more rarely experienced, one feels the presence of Christ himself.

Ordinarily Bernard followed the prevailing practice of regarding the Church as the Bride of Christ. But not always. Sometimes the Bride is the soul of the individual Christian. He then usually refers to Christ, not as the man Jesus, but in Johannine terminology as the Word of God. This is spelled out with a caution in these words:

> Take heed that you bring chaste ears to this discourse of love; and when you think of these two lovers, remember always that not a man and a woman are to be thought of, but the Word of God and a soul. And if I shall speak of Christ and the Church, the sense is the same, except that under the name of the Church is specified not one soul only, but the united souls of many, or rather their unanimity.[20]

In an unusually beautiful passage Bernard describes his own experience as an indication of how the Word—or the Bridegroom, he uses both terms—comes to the individual soul.

But now let me try to tell you of my own experience, as I set out to do. I speak as a fool; and yet I must admit that the Word has come even to me, and that many times. But never, when He has thus entered into me, have I perceived the actual moment of His coming. I have felt that He was present; I remember afterwards that He was then with me; and sometimes I have sensed His coming in advance. But never have I been aware of the particular moment when He came or went. Whence He came from into my soul, or whither He goes on leaving me, or by what road He enters or departs, I know not even now. Certainly it was not by my eyes that He entered, for He has no colour; nor was it by my ears, for He made not a sound. Neither was it my nostrils that discerned His presence, for His sweetness mingles with the mind, not with the air. The sense of taste did not detect Him either, for He is nothing that one eats or drinks; and touch was likewise powerless to apprehend Him, for He is utterly intangible. How, then, did He come in? Or did He *not* come in, perhaps, because He never was outside? For He is not one of the things that exist exteriorly to us. And yet how can I say that He comes from within me, when I know that in me there is nothing that is good? I have ascended to the highest in myself, and lo! the Word was towering far above it. My curiosity has led me to explore my lowest depths as well, only to find that He went deeper yet. If I looked out from myself, I saw Him stretching farther than the farthest I could see; and if I looked within, He was more inward still. So I recognized the truth of the apostle's words, "In Him we live and move and are." [21]

Bernard's problem is that of the person of any era, including our own, who attempts to find God through the senses. But his solution is ours also, in terms of an inward assurance which bears fruits in life. He continues:

You ask, then, how I knew that He was present, since His ways are past finding out? Because the Word is living and effective, and as soon as ever He has entered into me, He has aroused my sleeping soul, and stirred and softened and pricked my heart, that hitherto was sick and hard as stone. He has begun to pluck up and destroy, to build and to plant, to water the dry places and shed light upon the dark, to open what was shut, to warm the chill, to make the crooked straight and the rough places plain; so that my soul has blessed the Lord and all that is within me praised His holy Name. Thus has the Bridegroom entered into me; my senses told me nothing of His coming, I knew that He was present only by the movement of my heart; I perceived His power, because it put my sins to flight and exercised a strong control on all my impulses. I have been moved to wonder at His wisdom too, uncovering my secret faults and teaching me to see their sinfulness; and I have experienced His gentleness and kindness in such small measure of amendment as I have achieved; and, in the renewal and remaking of the spirit of my mind—that is, my inmost being, I have beheld to some degree the beauty of His glory and have been filled with awe as I gazed at His manifold greatness.[22]

Seldom has there been a more eloquent, and at the same time humble, witness to the moral and spiritual effects of companionship with Christ. Let him who will call such a passage erotic! It has, of course, been long contended that the celibate state of the monks and nuns caused them to translate their sexual fantasies into religious terms. But this charge is difficult to sustain in view of the spiritual purity of such writing as this. What they did was to take the highest human relationship they could envisage and use its imagery to the glory of God.

In many passages throughout Bernard's writings, he stresses the humanity of Jesus and calls upon Christians to imitate him. It is this which he regards as the center of the Christian life. Far more than his predecessors, he put the imitation of Christ in the foreground of his preaching. The traits which he emphasized most were the humility and love of Jesus, thus enjoined upon his followers. These two notes are sounded again and again in his preaching and writing, until they have been regarded as summing up his message.

In a treatise which there is not space here to comment on in any detail, *The Steps of Humility,* he demonstrated an unusual psychological as well as religious insight. It is based on the Benedictine Rule, and the twelve steps of humility are treated as the adverse of the temptations to pride.

This ability to combine psychological with spiritual discernment appears again in full force in his *On the Love of God.* This, he says, appears in the Christian in four stages, though he doubts that the fourth is fully possible in this mortal life. The first is that in which one loves himself for his own sake, encumbered with the cares of the body and its carnal desires. Yet even so, one must listen to the command of God to love his neighbor, and try to love him "in God," as one whom God has made to share our human nature. The second stage, which emerges after we find ourselves unable to cope with the tribulations of life, is to love God for one's own sake in order to secure the deliverance and mastery that the love of God makes possible. The third, a more exalted and truly Christian stage, is to love God for his sake. At this point it will no longer be hard to fulfill the commandment of loving one's neighbor, for one truly loves God and in this way also loves the things which are God's. This is as far as most Christians ever get in this life, but in heaven and possibly for a brief moment on earth, one may love himself only for God's sake.

Bernard does not claim to have attained to this fourth stage himself. Yet he gives a description of it in the familiar mystical terms:

> Blessed and holy, I would say, is he to whom it has been given to experience such a thing in this mortal life at rare intervals or even once, and this suddenly and scarcely for the space of a single moment. In a certain manner to lose yourself as though you were not, and to be utterly unconscious of yourself and to be emptied of yourself and, as it were, brought to nothing, this pertains to heavenly intercourse, not to human affection.[23]

This may happen, Bernard admits, but what he is far more certain of is that the human will can come into union with the will of God. To illustrate this kind of union he uses some vivid symbolism.

> Just as a little drop of water mixed with a lot of wine seems entirely to lose its own identity, while it takes on the taste of wine and its color; just as iron, heated and glowing, looks very much like fire, having divested itself of its original and characteristic appearance; and just as air flooded with the light of the sun is transformed into the same splendor of light so that it appears not so much lighted up as to be light itself; so it will inevitably happen that in saints every human affection will then, in some ineffable manner, melt away from self and be entirely transfused into the will of God.[24]

To sum up, Bernard had an extraordinary sense of what the presence of Christ can mean in human experience. He saw and enjoined the demands of humility and love as these come to us in Jesus. He discerned clearly both the limits of the human spirit in its natural state and its possibilities when lifted by and in response to the love of God. He found the mystical experience most attainably and most fully expressed in a sense of divine presence within a union of the human will with the will of God.

We do not ordinarily today use the symbolism of sex to express the soul's relation to its God. I do not recommend that we adopt this aspect of Bernard's thought. Yet a sex-ridden culture has something to learn from the chastity with which this saint of old turned it to the glory of God and the deepening of the life in Christ.

## 3. St. Francis

We turn now to a different type of mind and of action. St. Francis left so little writing that the citations will be few. What he left was an enduring message in the joyous simplicity, the utter dedication, and the fragrance of his life of prayer and service. He was a mystic, though not as the term is usually understood. His sainthood would be unquestioned even if he had not been canonized by the church.

He left two pieces of writing that are generally regarded as authentic, his "Hymn to the Sun," composed near the end of his life when he was already ill and blind, and his last testament pleading for the pure observance of his Rule against efforts to relax its requirements. I regret to have to say that the familiar prayer ascribed to him, "O Lord, make me an instrument of thy peace . . ." is probably not from his hand. But since it epitomizes so perfectly the spirit of his life, we may still continue to call it the prayer of St. Francis—the prayer of his heart. As with Jesus whose life he sought to imitate in love and service, we must see Francis through the eyes of those who loved him. Fortunately we have a number of early accounts of his life—one by Thomas of Celano almost immediately after his death and another later, one by Bonaventura a little later in the same century, the *Mirror of Perfection* and the *Little Flowers* in the next. We must expect to find miracles recounted in a credulous age, but the spirit of the man comes through with great clearness.

Born in the Umbrian town of Assisi in 1182, he was christened Giovanni Bernadone, but his father, a wealthy cloth merchant, seems to have changed his name to Francesco. He was a gay youth with an ebullient spirit and plenty of money to spend, and he was not much of a scholar. After being imprisoned in a war between Assisi and the neighboring Perugia and having an extended illness, he became restive in the attempt to find a purpose for his life. Praying one day in the church of St. Damian, he felt that the figure on the crucifix above him was calling him to a new way of life. "And whilst he was thus moved, straightway . . . the painted image of Christ Crucified spoke to him from out its pictured lips. And calling him by his name, "Francis," it said, "go, repair My house, the which as thou seest is falling into decay.'" [25] Presently he felt impelled to kiss the hands of lepers, from whom he had formerly shrunk in disgust and loathing, to serve in the lazarhouse, and to exchange his rich garments with those of a beggar. His father, much disturbed, brought him before the bishop of Assisi, whereupon the young Francis stripped off his clothes, threw down his purse of money, and declared that henceforth his sole allegiance was to his Father in heaven.

The call that shaped the direction of his later life came to him at Mass in the Church of Saint Mary of the Angels when he heard the priest read the opening words of the ninth chapter of Luke. From this time until his death at the early age of forty-four, Francis was to follow this mandate, preaching the gospel, serving those in need, living in poverty, loving God and man and all God's creatures, gathering followers about him and living in joyous, holy obedience. His faith lent courage to his actions, enough to go with a few followers to Rome to seek and obtain the blessing of Pope Innocent III upon his Rule, and to go to Egypt to try, though unsuccessfully, to convert the Moslem Soldan to Christianity.

Rivalry and sharp differences of opinion broke out between Francis and some of his trusted followers, and he was to discover the pain of internal dissension when the power struggle makes inroads upon idealism. The movement split apart into two groups—the *Spirituali,* who wished to keep to the original vows of simplicity and poverty, and the *Conventuali,* led by Friar Elias, who wished to make of the Order a more lax and worldly institution. The deep sorrow which this caused Francis probably hastened his death.

A more joyous feature of the movement was the establishment of a sisterhood under the leadership of the Lady Clare. She was a wealthy girl of noble birth who under Francis' preaching renounced a life of prestige and comfort, and with his help established a convent near St. Damian's chapel. This was to become the Second Order of St. Francis, which still exists.

Francis preached with such a vital message that multitudes flocked to hear him. To make provision for these people, most of whom could not leave their homes and ordinary occupations, he established what came to be known as the Third Order of St. Francis. These were originally called Penitents, and their vows have been thus summed up:

> The Penitent vowed to make restitution of all ill-gotten gain, to become reconciled with his enemies, to live in peace and concord with all men, to pass his life in prayer and works of charity, to keep certain fasts and vigils, to pay tithes regularly to the Church, to take no oath save under exceptional conditions, never to wear arms, to use no foul language, and to practise piety to the dead.[26]

These vows epitomize the moral and social aspects of Francis' preaching, all centered in conversion or fresh commitment to the Christian life. Among these requirements he was deeply concerned with peace-making and the ministry of reconciliation. One of his early biographers says this of him:

> The whole matter of his discourse was directed to the quenching of hatred and the establishment of peace. His dress was mean, his person insignificant, his face without beauty. But with so much power did God inspire his words that many noble families, sundered by ancient blood feuds, were reconciled for ever.[27]

However much overstated, this message still has relevance in a day greatly in need of "the quenching of hatred and the establishment of peace."

Yet such strenuous labors, in conjunction with rigorous living and the malaria and eye infection contracted in Egypt, wore out Francis' frail body. In 1224 he retired to the mountain hermitage of La Verna, and there he experienced the famous stigmata of Christ's crucifixion. The next summer in a solitary hut near St. Damian's, very ill and surrounded with vermin, he composed the "Hymn to the Sun." He lived on for a time in spite of repeated bleedings and other mistreatments by the physicians of his time, wrote his last testament, and died in 1226. The visitor to Assisi today may still see his burial-place in the crypt of the massive basilica which Friar Elias had erected over it a few years after his death—the last thing the Little Brother of the Poor would have wanted to be done.

Such were the external events connected with the life of one who has long been regarded as the most winsome, tender, and

Christlike of all the saints. We must now ask, "Does he give a lasting witness to our time?"

Can we today be "wedded to Lady Poverty" and go forth as joyous troubadours of God? Certainly not just as Francis did, though to his credit it should be said that he urged his followers to earn their own living and to beg for alms only in cases of necessity. Yet in our materialistic, money-centered society, the call to put self-denial, simplicity of living, and service to God and man at the center of life is not something to be scorned. Three men often regarded as twentieth-century saints, Albert Schweitzer, Toyohiko Kagawa, and Mahatma Gandhi, have done this and the world honors even when it does not imitate them.

Furthermore, centuries before the terms were coined Francis advocated and called on his followers to practice "the priesthood of all believers" and "the ministry of the laity." He did this with no aspersions on the priesthood of the church, but with a great sense of the mission Christ sets before every Christian. In this he is the Protestant's saint as well as the Catholic's.

What of his conversion? And the voice from the crucifix? Was he insane in his mingling with lepers and beggars, as his father believed he was? Whatever may have happened, Christ spoke to him and the message penetrated his soul. Every person who comes into the Christian life does so by way of his own temperament and his particular circumstances, and this was Francis' way. His conversion may perhaps be located at the moment when he was praying beneath the crucifix, but it had a before and after. A new unity brought both peace and fresh imperatives to a divided self, and what ensued was a total reorientation of his universe. What his biographers regarded as the miracle of a Voice from the crucifix, and later the miracle of the stigmata, can be accounted for psychologically, but the greatest miracle is Francis himself. It is to be found in what he became and what he did, and in what his memory has continued to do even to the present day. Let us not romanticize him—he had his faults and certainly his flaws of judgment. Yet he merits the enduring tributes the world has given him.

And what of Francis' preaching to the birds, which everybody knows about who knows anything at all about him? The account has it that he had been preaching to men and women, and had bidden the twittering swallows to keep still while he talked.

Then as he passed on he saw a large number of birds in the trees and some on the ground, so he decided to preach to them. Those in the trees came down to listen, and this was the substance of the sermon as the *Little Flowers* reports it:

My little sisters the birds, much are ye beholden to God your Creator, and alway and in every place ye ought to praise Him for that He hath given you a double and a triple vesture; He hath given you freedom to go into every place, and also did preserve the seed of you in the ark of Noe, in order that your kind may not perish from the earth. Again, ye are beholden to Him for the element of air which He hath appointed for you; moreover, ye sow not, neither do ye reap, and God feedeth you and giveth you the rivers and the fountains for your drink; He giveth you the mountains and the valleys for your refuge, and the tall trees wherein to build your nests, and forasmuch as ye can neither spin nor sew God clotheth you, you and your children: wherefore your Creator loveth you much, since he hath dealt so bounteously with you; and therefore beware, little sisters mine, of the sin of ingratitude, but ever strive to praise God.[28]

Not a bad sermon, were it addressed to humans! As it ended, Francis made the sign of the cross over the birds, and they flew away toward the east, west, south, and north. The story ends with these words:

. . . so the preaching of Christ's cross, renewed by St. Francis, was, through him and his friars, to be borne throughout the whole world; the which friars possessing nothing of their own in this world, after the manner of birds, committed their lives wholly to the providence of God.

The conclusion suggests strongly its allegorical nature. The concern of Francis for all living things, that is, his "reverence for life" in a familiar modern term, and even for inanimate nature as God's creation, marks him as a nature-mystic. But it is nature-mysticism in a deeply Christian context. His joy in nature and his joy in the Lord as its source are hardly distinguishable from each other. This becomes clear in his hymn of praise to Brother Sun, Sister Moon and the stars, Brother Wind, Sister Water, our Sister Mother Earth, and even our Sister Bodily Death, which he seems to have added shortly before his own dying. Yet this sense of complete kinship with nature never led him, as it has often led others, to identify nature with God or to forsake the church, its Christian imperatives, or its sacraments.

So, let us not try too hard to classify him. There has not been another quite like him. In a world very different from that of Francesco Bernadone, but with the same deep human needs and the same presence of God throughout all creation, the appeal of this spirit lives on. Let us hope that it may never cease to charm and to challenge us.

# V

# The Fertile Fourteenth Century

The fourteenth century was a great period in what Rufus Jones has aptly called, in a book bearing this title, "the flowering of mysticism." If we include in it *The Imitation of Christ,* which stands on the border between this and the following century, no other era has produced so much in the way of mystical interest and enduring devotional writing.

No longer was Italy or the south of Europe the primary source of this concern, though it was the century of Dante and great works of art. In mystical and devotional writing the torch passed northward, mainly to Germany and the Netherlands and to a less extent to England. In part there are discernible reasons for this movement. The Renaissance was burgeoning, and while in Italy this took the form of great advances in art and architecture there was little suggestion of a break with Rome. To the north the groundwork was already being laid in an accent on the individual's approach to God rather than on sacramental salvation or the power of the ecclesiastical structure. None of the mystics of this period left the church, but they did not make it the primary focus of the religious life. That lay within the soul and its sense of the divine Presence. Furthermore, the intellectual ferment of the Renaissance with its emphasis on classical learning and cultural values was introducing a note not unlike the secular mood of the present. In the next century it was to produce such satires on the church as those of Ulrich von Hutten and Erasmus of Rotterdam, but in the fourteenth the reaction to it was a stronger defense of personal religion.

## 1. A Rapid Survey

The limits of space prevent any extended discussion of most of these writings. In Thomas S. Kepler's *Fellowship of the Saints,* an excellent anthology of selected excerpts from the entire sweep of Christian devotional literature, fourteen writers from this century are included. I shall name each of them with a brief comment to locate them; then deal at some length with a few of the most influential.

There was the anonymous author of *The Mirror of Simple Souls* who wrote in French about 1300 to exalt the place of love in the soul. There was Johannes Eckhart, better known as Meister Eckhart, a German of great intellectual ability and deep devotional insight whose work is increasingly quoted in the modern world. There was Richard Rolle, an Englishman who exalted the love of God and of Jesus above the love of temporal things. There was Johannes Tauler, a Dominican monk and great German preacher who combined a very practical love of humanity with a spiritual love of God. There was Heinrich Suso, who along with Eckhart and Tauler became a leader of the "Friends of God" movement, and made of mysticism a very intimate personal experience. There was Jan van Ruysbroeck, a Flemish saint who with the spirit of St. Francis loved everybody and all God's creatures and carried this outgoing joy into the little community that gathered about him. There was Rulman Merswin, a Strasbourg banker who purchased an island, known as Green Isle, as a retreat center and opened it to both clergy and laity. Some important mystical writings were produced or compiled there, of which the authorship is uncertain. And there was the author of the anonymous but extraordinary *Theologia Germanica.*

Turning to England we find the author of another anonymous work, *The Cloud of Unknowing,* which bears strong marks of the *Mystical Theology* of Dionysius. There was Walter Hilton, an Augustinian canon whose work, *The Scale of Perfection,* shows with considerable psychological insight the upward steps toward divine communion. There was Juliana of Norwich, a Benedictine nun whose *Revelations of Divine Love* recounts her earlier experiences of visions and auditions, while her more mature emphasis is on penitence and divine grace. Another remarkable English woman of this period was Margery Kempe, a wife, mother, and extensive traveler, whose spiritual autobiography indicates acquaintance with numerous earlier mystical writings. To turn attention southward again to Italy, we find Catherine of Siena, an amazing woman who was a politician as well as a contemplative Dominican nun, and who exercised enough influence in public life to bring the papacy back from Avignon to Rome.

Finally we come to the most famous and influential devotional writing of this period, perhaps one of the greatest of Christian history outside the Bible, *The Imitation of Christ*. Who wrote it? We do not know, in spite of the fact that the name of Thomas à Kempis has long been associated with it. The consensus now appears to be that it is the spiritual diary of Gerhard Groote, the founder of the "Brethren of the Common Life" and a Dutch preacher toward the end of the fourteenth century, but was edited with some additions by à Kempis around the middle of the next.

We must now center attention on some of the most important of these writings. Yet as we look at the group as a whole certain traits stand out. Devotional writing has largely emerged from the cloister into the common life. It centers more in the demands of the Christian way for daily life than in rare and ecstatic states. Its self-negation is tempered with a very positive love of God and with the duty of service to others. This trend, with some exceptions here and there, was to become the dominant trend in Christian mysticism in later centuries.

## 2. Meister Eckhart

We must look first at the most philosophical and the most influential of the mystics of this period, who gathered up in his thought a great succession from the past, yet with a high degree of originality influenced his own and later centuries. He is even today widely quoted for his practical injunctions to the devotional life. Yet his major contribution lies in his philosophical system, from which it is less easy to cite clear and fruitful quotations. I hesitate to attempt to interpret it in a few pages, yet the attempt must be made.

Johannes Eckhart was born about 1260, though his exact birth date is not known. Well along in his career, about 1303, he received the degree of Master of Sacred Theology from the University of Paris, and from this fact and his acknowledged intellectual acumen the title has stuck. Like Augustine and Bernard, he lived a very active life. He was a Dominican monk, the prior of his order at Erfurt, provincial vicar of Thuringia, and later vicar-general of Bohemia. He traveled widely, preached frequently in German both in the cloisters and to the multitudes who heard him eagerly, and wrote learned treatises in both Latin and German. We owe the preservation of many of his sermons to some Dominican nuns who transcribed them as he spoke or wrote them down from memory.

Though Eckhart remained a loyal churchman in his personal attitudes and relations, he fell into disfavor with Rome. He was charged with "guilt by association" with the Beghards and the Brethren of the Free Spirit, who like the Quakers of a later day found their way to God through the Inner Light rather than ecclesiastical channels. More serious, however, were the charges of pantheism in his teachings. These accusations of heresy were under investigation when he died in 1327. Two years later a Papal Bull condemned twenty-eight propositions drawn from his writings. Seventeen of these were deemed heretical and the other eleven rash and unwise, with the comment that he "wished to know more than he should."

Though Eckhart thought of himself not as contradicting but as interpreting the tenets of Christian faith, we shall note some semi-pantheistic tendencies in his teaching. But, first, let us note the practicality of his ideas about the Christian's devotional life. It required the complete subordination of the self to God, but this was a demand on the whole of life, not for special occasions only. He had no place for raptures and ecstasies as a substitute for human service, as is seen in his often quoted statement, "Even if one were in a rapture like St. Paul's and there was a sick man who needed help, I think it would be far better to come out of the rapture and show love by serving the needy one." [1] He loved silence and meditation, too seldom available for long in his busy life, but he believed that the true test of the inward life is found in its outward expressions. On this basis he ranked Martha above Mary. Said he, "God's purpose in the union of contemplations is fruitfulness in works; for in contemplation thou servest thyself alone, but the many in good works." [2] Yet he was as sure as Luther was to be later that good works alone would not impart salvation. "God is no more to be found in any bodily exercise than He is to be found in sin. . . .

The beginning of the holy life is to be found in the inner man, in vision and in loving." [3]

With this recognition that not all of what Eckhart wrote was as abstruse as much of it seems, let us look at the outlines of his system. That the Dominican nuns could have understood him enough to write down his sermons is no small tribute to their ability!

Eckhart stood in the succession of Plotinus and Dionysius, of Augustine and Bernard. Dante was his contemporary. Thomas Aquinas was his immediate predecessor, having died when Eckhart was a boy of fourteen. He not only knew the Neoplatonists but also Aristotle by way of Aquinas and the Moslem strand through Averroës. He built on these foundations but added an original superstructure. Though he probably had no direct contact with the Orient, his thought has been likened by Rudolf Otto in *Mysticism, East and West* to that of the great Hindu philosopher Sankara, and to Buddhist mysticism in D. T. Suzuki's *Mysticism: Christian and Buddhist.*

Though its elements are interwoven, Eckhart's thought may be summarized for convenience under four topics: (1) the Godhead and God; (2) the human soul; (3) the eternal generation of the Son; (4) the Eternal Now and its relation to the world of time and space.

It will be recalled that in Plotinus the Ultimate Reality is the Source, or the One, known only though emanations as Mind and Soul, and that in Dionysius God is the Divine Darkness, unknown in his essential nature though Christian terms may be applied as symbols. Eckhart followed this Neoplatonic route in his conception of the Godhead, but with a different approach to the problem of our knowledge. The Godhead is the Source, the Fount—but since we cannot know this through the senses or human reason he (or it) is Emptiness, a "desert" and a "barren wilderness." How then do we know Him? Through God, who is the Christian Trinity of Father, Son, and Holy Spirit. The Father is the Creator of all that is; the Son is the Word (the Logos) pervading all things; the Holy Spirit is known through love. Thus the Christian can speak of God as having personality, power, righteousness, love and other attributes. He is not left in darkness, for it is the unitary but threefold God that makes the bridge from the unknown and empty Godhead to the point where we are.

Eckhart's doctrine of the human soul has lasted to the present, and is reaffirmed whenever one speaks of a Divine Spark within each of us. He calls it the Fünklein, the Apex, the Center, the Ground, a divine Light, a Ray of divinity, Innermost Essence, Bottomless Abyss. Whatever his various names for it, he believed that in every human soul there is something of the very nature of God. Here it is that the human soul meets God.

Again and again Eckhart affirms the nearness of God within the soul. "Thou needst not seek Him here or there, for He is no further off than the door of thy heart." "I am as certain as I live that nothing is as close to me as God. God is nearer to me than I am to my own self." "When the soul enters into her Ground, into the innermost recesses of her being, divine power suddenly pours into her." [4] Had he been content to make such assertions as these, he might not have got into trouble with the authorities. But he did not stop with affirming God's nearness, and in other passages he seems to affirm the identity of God and man. We find him saying, "When I saw into myself I saw God in me." "Where God is there is the soul, and where the soul is there is God." "To gauge the soul we must gauge her with God, for the Ground of God and the Ground of the soul are one nature." [5] It is not surprising that the ecclesiastical dogmatists scented a pantheistic heresy in such statements. But the one that clinched this position as a blasphemous self-deification was, "The eye with which I see God is the same as that with which He sees me." [6]

I doubt that Eckhart intended a pantheistic identification of the human soul with God, any more than does the Quaker or other Christian of today who endeavors to discern and follow the leading of the Inner Light. He disclaims such identity when he says, following Aquinas, "The soul is contained in a place, as it were, betwixt time and eternity, touching them both." [7] He was struggling with the perennial problem of how to affirm the utter transcendence yet the immediate immanence of God, and he was unguarded in his language.

Eckhart is somewhat inconsistent as to whether this divine Center within the soul is God or the Godhead. He uses both terms, but seems to have reserved the latter mainly for the union of the soul with God in the mystical consciousness. In speaking of the imitation of Christ he distinguishes between "the way of the manhood," which is incumbent upon all Christians, and "the way of the Godhead," which is for the mystic only. Into the Godhead one may carry no sensory images or concern with the things of time and space. In vivid imagery he says, "Into the naked Godhead none may get except he himself be as naked as he was when he was spilt out from God." [8] Elsewhere he says, "God is with us in our inmost soul provided He find us within and not gone out on business with our five senses." [9]

The Son must, of course, be the incarnation of God in Jesus Christ. But the Christ figures in Eckhart's thought much more than Jesus. So by the eternal generation of the Son he means, first, the coming to birth in a cosmic sense of all creatures through the Spirit of Life which is the Logos. Here he enunciates a principle which extends from Stoic through Johannine to current process theology. All created things, and not the human soul only, reflect their divine origin and God's presence.

But he means more than this: what Eckhart is most concerned to stress by this term is the conscious birth of the Son within the human soul. In the birth of Jesus, the son of Mary, is the pattern and supreme instance of what God the Father is doing eternally. The meeting of cosmic and eternal with temporal birth is thus epitomized in a Christmas sermon of his, "We are celebrating the feast of the Eternal Birth which God the Father has borne and never ceases to bear in all Eternity: whilst this birth also comes to pass in Time and in human nature." But immediately he adds, "But if it takes not place in me, what avails it? Everything lies in this, that it should take place in me." [10] In another place he says, "When the soul brings forth the Son, it is happier than Mary." [11]

Does Eckhart mean by the birth of the Son within the soul what is usually called rebirth, that is, a conversion experience? Or something of a more mystical nature? He does not draw a sharp line at this point, and it is an indication of his view of the totality of the Christian life that he does not. What he does do is to offer guidance as to how to come to this birth.

How, then, does the birth of the Son within the soul come about? Eckhart is orthodox enough to say that it comes by grace as the act of God. Yet at the same time he insists that the soul must make preparation for it. As soon as the soul is ready, the birth will take place. "God is bound to act, to pour Himself into thee, as soon as ever He shall find thee ready." [12] This readiness comes from withdrawal from the things of space and time that split up our lives to enter into the unitary depths where God already dwells within us. This requires quiet and solitude, and the use of intellect and love to go beyond the claims of both intellect and the senses. With his usual vivid style we find Eckhart saying, "Up, noble soul, put on thy jumping shoes, understanding and love, and leap the workings of thy powers: leap thine own understanding, . . . and spring into the heart of God, into his hiddenness, wherein thou art hidden from all creatures." [13] By this leap into the God within the soul, Eckhart seems not to advocating either asceticism or self-induced spiritual raptures, but a life of self-renunciation, trust in God, and fulfillment within life's vicissitudes.

The Eternal Now is the eternal God within the world and the soul of man, and therefore a God-filled present that is vastly more full of meaning than the passing moment in the space-time world. History as something remembered from the past and projected into the future seems not to have meant a great deal to Eckhart. He believed that Jesus lived and died and rose again as recorded in the Scriptures, and he declares, "The best thing God ever did for man was to become man himself." [14] Yet in his thought the Jesus of history is subordinate to the indwelling and eternal Christ. Likewise heaven, hell, and purgatory became to him present states within the individual soul—another startling statement that exposed him to attack by the Establishment.

To understand the Eternal Now as Eckhart conceived it, it is necessary to take into account the Neoplatonic background of his thought. In current diction the term is often used without this background, and thus it makes less sense than he made of it. But from his frame of reference, the world of time and space with its ever-changing phenomena is not the real world. The true Reality is eternal and changeless, and the space-time world, though derived from it, reflects it imperfectly like shadows in a cave or changing images in a mirror. The real world is *That Which Is,* as Augustine called it: it is the Changeless. It has no before and after, or movement through the processes of history.

Thus Eternity is not simply an infinitely long period of time; it is *timeless*. Yet the Eternal impinges on the temporal at every moment and can be experienced by the receptive mind and soul.

What are we to think of this massive system? I cannot go all the way with Eckhart's thought. Much as we must confess silence before the mystery of God, a faceless Godhead behind the God we know through Christ is not necessary and is not helpful. The human soul does, indeed, have a depth of kinship to God that gives it receptivity to the divine presence; yet man remains man and God is God. It is the eternal, living Christ that meets us in the rebirth within us of the Son; yet we should not be calling him Son, nor do we have the guidance we need for Christian living, without the earthly ministry of Jesus. God is the eternal and ever-present One, changeless in His own nature; yet with long purposes which must be fulfilled within our earth-bound world of time and space.

Though we need not follow Eckhart in his total system, from his writings two dominant impressions emerge. One of these is the range and power of his thought, in which he wrestles with still current problems and proposes solutions not unlike some being set forth in the present. The other impression is the warmth and spiritual realism of his assurances and injunctions for Christian living. With a few of these I must close this survey.

What I thank him for is for not being able of his goodness to leave off loving me.

No man ever wanted anything so much as God wants to make the soul aware of him. God is ever ready, but we are so unready . . . God is in, we are out; God is at home, we are strangers.

A life of rest and peace in God is good; a life of pain in patience is still better; but to have peace in a life of pain is best of all.

I say that next to God there is no nobler thing than suffering. . . . If anything were nobler than suffering, God would have saved mankind therewith.

As long as the soul has not thrown off all her veils, however thin, she is unable to see God.

Art thou looking for God, seeking God with a view to thy personal good, thy personal profit? Then in truth thou art not seeking God.

If thou seekest aught of thine thou never shalt find God, for thou art not seeking God merely. Thou art seeking something with God, making a candle of God, as it were, with which to find something, and then, having found it, throwing the candle away.

There are plenty to follow our Lord half-way, but not the other half.[15]

Some of these injunctions must inevitably seem like strong medicine. But Eckhart was not the man to apply mild poultices to souls in need of healing by the love of God! And no preacher or devotional writer was ever more sure of the love of God than he. His contemporaries called him "a man from whom God hid nothing." We can hardly say that. Yet a glow still shines from his luminous soul to light our path today.

## 3. John Tauler

In spite of the pressures of space I must give at least two or three pages to another of the Friends of God, less original and less of an intellectual giant, but a great preacher whose pungent proclamation of the gospel is still relevant after six centuries. I recall that one of my students, fresh from writing a seminar paper on this man, exclaimed, "What wonderful sermons! They could be preached in my church today!" Tauler also merits a place in history from the fact that he had a strong influence on Martin Luther, less than the anonymous *Theologia Germanica* but earlier. Thus though he remained a loyal servant of the Roman Church to the end of his days, he helped to usher in the spirit of the Protestant Reformation.

Johannes Tauler was born in approximately 1300—the date of his birth is unknown and may have been somewhat earlier—and he died in 1361. Except for a brief period in Basel he spent all of his life in and around Strasbourg. He was a Dominican monk and a disciple of Eckhart, though it is uncertain whether he studied with him directly. A widely read and learned man, he was not a genius, save as he had a genius for discerning the heart of the Christian gospel. Evelyn Underhill says of him, "John Tauler, friar-preacher of Strassburg, was a born missionary: a man who combined with great theological learning and mystical genius of a high order an overwhelming zeal for souls." [16] Rufus Jones's appraisal is "that he was first of all a good man, a genuine man, a simple, humble Christian, exhibiting in life and action what he taught as gospel.[17] This combination of qualities explains why his sermons, which are his only authentic works that have been preserved, still ring true.

A dominant note in Tauler's thought is the need of unselfing, of following the way of the Cross through pain and suffering, and in Paul's terminology "dying into life." It was Tauler who was chiefly influential in the conversion of the rich Strasbourg banker Rulman Merswin, which led to the decision to use his wealth for the founding of the Green Isle Community as a place of spiritual retreat for the Friends of God. Yet Tauler pointed the way to a deeper and more authentic poverty of spirit than the renunciation of all earthly goods. Mortification was much more than the denial of bodily pleasures and comforts; it was coming into new life through self-surrender to God. Few more searching words than these have ever been written in explication of the Christian concept of dying into life:

> This dying has many degrees, and so has this life. A man might die a thousand deaths in one day and find at once a joyful life corresponding to each of them. This is as it must be: God cannot deny or refuse this to death. The stronger the death the more powerful and thorough is the corresponding life; the more intimate the death, the more inward the life. Each life brings strength, and strengthens to a harder death. When a man dies to a scornful word, bearing it in God's name, or to some inclination inward or outward, acting or not acting against his own will, be it in love or grief, in word or act, in going or staying; or if he denies his desires of taste or sight, or makes no excuses when wrongfully accused; or anything else, whatever it may be, to which he has not yet died, it is harder at first to one who is unaccustomed to it. . . . A great life makes reply to him who dies in earnest even in the least things, a life which strengthens him immediately to die a greater death; a death so long and strong, that it seems to him hereafter more joyful, good and pleasant to die than to live, for he finds life in death and light shining in darkness.[18]

Tauler was also very much aware of that state of the soul of which many of the mystics speak, and to which John of the Cross was later to give a lasting name, "the dark night of the soul." This is a sense of the absence of God, the loss of the soul's former peace and joy, the apparent relapse to lower spiritual levels. To most of the mystics, Tauler included, this was a form of divine purgation and a discipline by which they were led through to a better and stronger life. "Think not," says he, "that God will be always caressing His children, or shine upon their head, or kindle their hearts as He does at first. . . . We must now serve the Lord with strenuous industry and at our own cost." Yet not in vain, or without hope. He continues:

> Then first do we attain to the fulness of God's love as His children, when it is no longer happiness or misery, prosperity or adversity, that draws us to Him or keeps us back from Him. What we should then experience none can utter; but it would be something far better than when we were burning with the first flame of love, and had great emotion, but less true submission.[19]

Tauler in the main took over Eckhart's philosophy but with a more evangelical emphasis. He believed as did his mentor that there is in every person an uncreated divine Spark, its Apex, or as he more often called it, its Ground, the divine Abyss. This remains in darkness as long as one's eyes are too weak to behold it; then from it shines a divine Light which is the bearer of the grace of God. From John's Gospel he also calls it the inward Word. "The inward Word is so unutterably near to us inwardly, in the very principle of our being, that not even man himself, not even his own thought, is so nigh, or is planted so deep within him, as is the Eternal Word in man."[20]

Faithful and obedient churchman though he was, it was in this inward Word that he found the deepest spiritual reality. Though in an institutional sense it is inaccurate to call him a precursor of the Reformation, the entire Friends of God movement had an emphasis that was leading in this direction. Tauler dares to say:

> God is a lover of hearts and communes directly and not through anything external. . . . God desires an inner living love. There is more truth in such an one than in a man who sings so lustily that his song reaches heaven; or in anything that he can do by fasting or watching or anything else that is external.[21]

Tauler believed that the highest spiritual goal in life is the attainment of union with God in the inner depths of one's being. But this was to be tested, not by an emotional upheaval, but by the capacity to endure suffering and to act in love, compassion, and service toward others. Even in "stormy love" this anchor would hold, and the divine love within one would flow out to all men. The reciprocal nature of these loves becomes evident in these words:

> So long as thou hast a whole and undivided love toward all men, a share of the divine influences which God intends to bestow on all men will flow out through thee in this love of thine. The moment thou severest thyself from this spirit of universal love thou wilt miss this outflow of divine love which otherwise would fill thy vessel overbrimming full.[22]

Tauler's witness after six centuries indicates that he had within him much of this outflowing divine love. This is why "the common people heard him gladly." And why he is one of my favorites among all the mystics.

## 4. The *Theologia Germanica*

We come now to a famous mystical classic, one of the chief legacies of the Friends of God movement to posterity, the anonymous *Theologia Germanica.* Martin Luther gave it this name. When he discovered it, he was captured by it, and published a section of it in 1516 and the entire book in 1518. He said of it in his preface, "Next to the Bible and St. Augustine, no book hath ever come into my hands, whence I have learnt or would wish to learn more of what God, Christ, and man and all things are." Many editions of it have ensued, one of which a century later called it *A Golden Book of German Divinity,* a more colorful title. Yet the original designation has stuck.

Who was this nameless author? All that is known about him is from a manuscript discovered in 1850 which says that he was "of the Teutonic Order, a priest and warden of the house of the Teutonic Order in Frankfort." It is generally believed to have been written sometime during the second half of the fourteenth century. Anything else about the author has to be deduced from the book itself, which says much about personal religion but nothing of the author's personal history. Doubtless this is intentional, for its dominant note is the negation of self-will, and the author may have thought it inappropriate to claim credit for himself by placing his name upon it.

In contrast with Luther's high estimate of the book, Calvin called it "a bag of tricks produced by Satan's cunning to confound the whole simplicity of the Gospel." My judgment lies between these positions. The book is a gem of mystical literature, but is has some shortcomings.

It may be recalled that W. T. Stace holds that all mysticism is paradoxical.[23] While I think this is an overstatement with regard to the total sweep of mystical literature, it is certainly true of this book. When viewed from a sympathetic standpoint, all its major emphases may be taken as reinforcing the basic tenets of Christian faith and morality. When viewed more adversely, they seem to range close to pantheism in theology and to masochism in psychology. Apparently Luther read it from one of these points of view, Calvin from the other. There is no evidence of intentional inconsistency on the author's part. He seems to be trying to say as honestly as possible what the Christian faith as mediated through the Bible and the Eckhart tradition says to him.

We must try to look at it as objectively as possible. And let us begin with its primary note, the conquest and eradication of self-will. He rings the changes on the need to deny the claims of "the I, the me, the mine." "Nothing is contrary to God but self will." [24] "All deception beginneth in self-deception." [25] "But what is true obedience? I answer, that a man should so stand free, being quit of himself, that is, of his I, and Me, and Self, and Mine, and the like, that in all things, he should no more seek or regard himself, than if he did not exist, and should take as little account of himself as if he were not, and another had done all his works." [26]

The cause of the coming of sin into the world, says this author, is the self-will of Adam. "Had he eaten seven apples, and yet never claimed anything for his own, he would not have fallen: but as soon as he called something his own, he fell and would have fallen if he had never touched an apple." And so with Adam's successors. But wherein lies the remedy? In a simple yielding to God, which opens the way to divine grace. "And because I will not do so, but I count myself to be my own, and I say, 'I,' 'Mine,' 'Me,' and the like, God is hindered, so that He cannot do His work in me alone and without hindrance; for this cause my fall and my going astray remain unhealed. Behold! this all cometh of my claiming somewhat for my own." [27]

The most famous and often-quoted of all these sayings is "Nothing burneth in hell but self-will." [28] From this we are not to assume that the author denied the existence of an after-life. He certainly believed in a glorious life with God beyond the earthly pilgrimage, though he was noncommittal about hell as a place of future torment. But with a spiritual insight beyond that of most of his contemporaries, he knew that heaven and hell are present realities in the lives of persons.

So acute is his analysis of the mental states of a person buffeted by his own self-will that it may be profitable to quote him at some length.

> Christ's soul must needs descend into hell, before it ascended to heaven. So must also the soul of man. But mark ye in what manner this cometh to pass. When a man truly perceiveth and considereth himself, who and what he is, and findeth himself utterly vile and wicked, and unworthy of all the comfort and kindness that he hath ever received from God, or from the creatures, he falleth into such a deep abasement and despising of himself that he thinketh himself unworthy that the earth should bear him, and it seemeth to him reasonable that all creatures in heaven and earth should rise up against him and avenge their Creator on him, and should punish and torment him; and that he were unworthy even of that. . . .
>
> Now God hath not forsaken a man in this hell, but He is laying His hand upon him, that the man may not desire nor regard anything but the Eternal Good only. . . . And then, when the man neither careth for, nor seeketh, nor desireth, anything but the Eternal Good alone, and seeketh not himself, nor his own things, but the honor of God only, he is made a partaker of all manner of joy, bliss, peace, rest and consolation, and so the man is henceforth in the Kingdom of Heaven.
>
> This hell and this heaven are two good, safe ways for a man in this present time, and happy is he who truly findeth them. . . .
>
> And when a man is in one of these two states, all is right with him, and he is as safe in hell as in heaven, and so long as a man is on earth, it is possible for him to pass ofttimes from the one into the other. . . . But when the man is in neither of these two states he holdeth converse with the creature, and wavereth hither and thither, and knoweth not what manner of man he is. Therefore he shall never forget either of them, but lay up remembrance of them in his heart.[29]

Does this sound antiquated? It can hardly be said of contemporary man that he is as conscious of his own sin as this passage would suggest. Yet it is not at all unusual to "hold converse with the creature," and as a result to "waver hither and thither" without inner stability. The author's position is far removed from the secular self-acceptance and advocacy of self-love that are popular goals today, but in his understanding of sin as egocenticity and grace as a divine gift he is on firm ground.

In justice to this unknown author, he never sets forth the conquest of self-will as an end in itself; it is that God may abound in the life of the soul. "Now where a creature or a man forsaketh and cometh out of himself and his own things, there God entereth in with His own, that is with Himself." [30] "The more the Self, the I, the Me, the Mine, that is, self-seeking and selfishness abate in a man, the more doth God's I, that is, God Himself, increase in him." [31] This blending of the human soul with God comes to its fullest expression in an often quoted passage, "I would fain be to the Eternal Goodness, what his own hand is to a man." [32]

Is this pantheism? On the one hand, it is no more pantheistic than "I am the vine; you are the branches." Yet the author has been charged with deifying man because he says, "He who is imbued with or illuminated by the Eternal or divine Light, and inflamed or consumed with Eternal or divine love, he is a god-like man and a partaker of the divine nature." [33] It seems unlikely that he ever thought of himself as doing more than to announce sound Christian doctrine. In any case he is less open to the charge of pantheism than Eckhart, for he is more noncommittal as to whether the center of the soul is created or uncreated. "The true light is that Eternal Light which is God; or else it is a created light, but yet divine, which is called grace." [34] He was content to leave it at that.

It is clear that the author's protest against self-seeking and self-centeredness, rigorous though it is, has a Christian base. Its foundation is self-denial and the way of the Cross. What it lacks is the imperative to use many sources of personal growth for the sake of the fullest service to God and other persons. This must be supplied from other angles. Yet, despite this lack, it contains a wealth of wisdom.

## 5. The Fruitage of the Century

With reluctance I must bypass several other great figures of this marvelous era of the outpouring of the Spirit in mystical devotion. Yet a few of them who stand in a particular succession must be looked at a little further than was possible in the preliminary survey.

Jan van Ruysbroeck (1293-1381), the greatest of the Flemish saints, was a follower of Eckhart in his intellectual system, but his major service lay in a clear and vital witness to spiritual realities. In addition to various tracts he wrote eleven books, with such arresting titles as *The Book of the Kingdom of God's Lovers, The Book of the Spiritual Tabernacle, The Adornment of the Spiritual Marriage,* and *The Book of Supreme Truth.* Evelyn Underhill says of him, "In Ruysbroeck's works the metaphysical and personal aspects of mystical truth are fused and attain their highest expression. Intellectually indebted to St. Augustine, Richard of St. Victor and Eckhart, his value lies in the fact that the Eckhartian philosophy was merely the medium by which he expressed the results of profound experience." [35]

Ruysbroeck's life story is uneventful. It demonstrates that greatness can emerge from the most simple surroundings and cast its light forward through the centuries. He was born in a small village near Brussels, and spent his adolescent years with an uncle as a spiritual guide. He somewhere—it is uncertain where—absorbed enough education to become a parish priest and to write books that reflect familiarity with the mystical tradition from Dionysius through Augustine to Eckhart. At the age of fifty, with the uncle and the uncle's friend, he became virtually a hermit in a little community which they formed for the cultivation of the spiritual life. There in the midst of beautiful natural surroundings he wrote his books, participating in meditation and in the ordinary household tasks, and gradually drawing about him a circle of devoted disciples. There he remained for thirty-eight years, happily serving God in an unpretentious way.

One of those who visited this little community and were captured by its spirit was Gerhard Groote of whom we must speak presently, for Ruysbroeck passed on through him an undying flame. But before leaving Ruysbroeck let us look at one quotation.

Ruysbroeck took over from Eckhart the idea of the inaccessible and unknowable God in his essential nature, "Abyssmal," "Simple Nudity," "a pure, imageless Unity." But he could not leave his God in such vacuity. He took also the idea of the

Ground or Spark of divinity in the human soul by which God may be found and man may be purified by God's love. He was much more careful than Eckhart to make it clear that man's union with God is one of love and not of any metaphysical merging. This is evident in these words:

> That measureless love which is God Himself, dwells in the pure deeps of our spirit, like a burning brazier of coals. And it throws forth brilliant and fiery sparks which stir and enkindle heart and senses, will and desire, and all the powers of the soul, with a fire of love. . . . As air is penetrated by the brightness and heat of the sun, and iron is penetrated by fire; so that it works through fire the works of fire, since it burns and shines like the fire, . . . yet each of these keeps its own nature—the fire does not become iron, and the iron does not become fire, so likewise is God in the being of the soul. . . . The creature never becomes God nor does God ever become the creature.[36]

This certainty of God and his grace, and with it the certainty of the distinction between God and the creature, is relevant to vital issues in current theology. Without it, the immanentism or panentheism of process theology bogs down in pantheism. Some great thoughts came to expression in that little community of Groenendael (Green Vale) in the Belgian forest of Soignes!

Gerhard Groote (1340-1384) was born at Deventer in the Netherlands. Rufus Jones calls him the bridge between the Friends of God movement and new stirrings leading toward the Protestant Reformation—the last influential figure of the one movement and the first of the other.[37] Posterity is indebted to him for two historically certain developments and a third unproved but important possibility. He was the principal leader of a thrust toward reforming the Church through increasing the spiritual vitality of its members. This was called the "New Devotion." He was the progenitor of the "Brethren of the Common Life," an association of lay people without monastic vows who shared their possessions and a simple religious life, supporting themselves by their labors in the world. The third possibility—that Groote's spiritual diary is the chief cornerstone of *The Imitation of Christ*—is an unsettled question which has considerable evidence to support it.

Groote as a young man appeared to have everything in his favor, an excellent education, wealth, and a bright future. Tradition has it that his life was changed in its course by a small event with large consequences. When he was watching a public game one day in Cologne an unnamed stranger, believed to have been a Friend of God, approached him with the question, "Why art thou here? Thou ought to become another man." This word struck home. A visit to Ruysbroeck stirred him deeply and pointed the way to his becoming another man. He entered a Carthusian monastery where he spent three years in somewhat ascetic practices but also "carefully tilling the field of his own heart" and "wiping away the mildew of his old life and restoring the image of his inner man to purity." [38]

He emerged to become a lay preacher of much power, choosing this to the priesthood as bringing him nearer to the people. Others joined him in the New Devotion, but his was the most prophetic voice. In his effort to reform the Church through the inward reformation of its people, he remained a loyal Catholic in his own faith and allegiance. Yet, as with Jesus, the revolutionary undercurrents of his preaching were detected. At the height of his evangelistic witness opposition arose, and his license to preach was revoked. This was a bitter blow. But it did not quench his spirit.

Groote then turned his attention to what was to become the Brethren of the Common Life. While he was the movement's energizing spirit he did not live to complete its organization, which was done by his disciple and co-worker, Florentius Radewyn. Brother-houses and some sister-houses were established. The movement exerted a valuable influence in Holland and Germany, rendering practical service through its schools for the common people, disseminating religious influence, and copying manuscripts in its brother-houses. Thomas à Kempis (1380-1471) was a member of this brotherhood, and Erasmus (1466-1536) was a product of one of its schools.

Thus the torch was being passed on from one of these Spirit-filled men to another. More than a half-century after Groote's death a manuscript was produced on which was written in Latin, "Finished and completed in the year of our Lord 1441 by the hand of brother Thomas van Kempen, at Mount Saint Agnes, near Zwolle." Does this mean that the mind as well as the hand of Thomas à Kempis created *The Imitation of Christ*? Or did he compile, edit, and copy some previous writing? The question is of no small importance, for it has become the most widely read devotional book outside the Bible and has passed through more than three thousand editions.

The answer is at best inconclusive, but if the second alternative is chosen, it is necessary to absolve the writer of any conscious plagiarism. There were no footnotes with references in those days. Whatever was written and seemed to have Christian truth belonged to the world for its edification. The same spirit that prompted the anonymity of the *Theologia Germanica* was doubtless in the mind of both Groote and à Kempis. To claim worldly honors for one's work would not have seemed fitting. This prodecure is baffling to historical research but has its Christian rationale.

All that can be said with certainty is that considerable portions of the *Imitation* were in circulation during the early part of the fifteenth century, long before 1441. There is no sure way to trace their sources. One of them is believed to be the spiritual diary of Groote, and it is enough like portions of the *Imitation* to indicate a connection. Furthermore, Thomas wrote a *Life of Gerard the Great* and this might well have familiarized him with Groote's writing. In any case, there is no need to dismiss him as a mere copyist, for if he compiled, edited, and gave its remarkable literary flavor to the manuscript, this achievement merits enduring fame.

Not much needs to be said of Thomas' long life. He was the son of John Haemmerlein of Kempen, near Cologne, but his true surname has given way to the place of his birth. He was educated at the school of the Brethren of the Common Life at Deventer, and as a young man was admitted to the Order of Canons Regular of that body, which by that time was no longer wholly a lay movement. He spent nearly all of his adult life at a monastery of the Brethren, first at Windesheim and then at Mount Saint Agnes near Zwolle in the Netherlands, where he served many years as sub-prior. He was an excellent copyist, Latin scholar, and student of the Scriptures. It is known that he tediously copied the entire Latin Bible, which may account somewhat for the frequency of quotations from the Bible which appear in the *Imitation*. He did other writing, including his life of Groote, but this one book, whatever his relation to it, is his great gift to posterity.

As for the book itself, it is both so many-faceted and so

familiar to most persons concerned with the devotional life that I shall not attempt a detailed analysis of it. It shows deep psychological as well as spiritual insight, and with many a pungent sentence which still arrests our attention it counsels humility, patience, trust in God, self-subordination at the call of God. It gives no specific chart for the imitation of Christ, but it is a call throughout to follow Christ and thus find peace and rest for the soul, even in the way of the Cross. It does not cover the whole gamut of Christian living, for it reflects the atmosphere of the cloister and says little of social action except in terms of injunctions to "let all men be loved for Jesus and Jesus for himself." [39] It is especially helpful in its understanding of spiritual dryness and "the dark night of the soul."

Some have questioned that the book is mystical literature, for it contains no ecstasies—only the calm joy of deep personal devotion to the will and way of Christ. I consider it mysticism of a very high order, and I never open it without finding something which "speaks to my condition." No book can contain everything which God says to the soul, but this one contains much.

So, in this book the fertile fourteenth century comes to its enduring fruitage. Though dated from the fifteenth, it sums up the message of the amazing one before it. The thinking, the speaking, the writing, and the living of the followers of Christ in those faraway days live after them to light our path today.

# VI

# Protestant Piety Emerges

Let it be clear that the term "piety" as it will be used in this chapter, and might well be used more commonly, is not the drab and lackluster religiosity often attached to the term. Piety in its best connotation means a deep Christian dedication which extends to the whole of life, a life made luminous and strong from the daily indwelling presence of the Holy Spirit. It ought to be a term of honor and not of opprobrium.

We have now traced the course of mystical and devotional writing through the spirit and words of some of the great creative figures of the early and medieval church, and have noted the amazing outpouring of spiritual insight in Germany and the Low Countries during the fourteenth century and the years that immediately followed. Although the spirit of Protestantism was brewing in these years, there was as yet no overt break with the Roman Church in either its institutional or sacramental aspects. This was to come with the cataclysmic events of the sixteenth century.

Many events preceding Luther's radical break with Rome led up to the Protestant Reformation. It would carry us too far afield from the main theme to try to discuss these in any detail. There were, of course, the manifest abuses in the Roman Church, of which the sale of indulgences to gather funds to build St. Peter's was only the most glaring symbol. Long before Luther set the whole movement ablaze by nailing his ninety-five theses on the door of the church at Wittenberg, these abuses were being recognized and uneasily accepted. There were rumblings of discontent against not only the evidences of moral decadence in the Church, but against a rigid institutional control over the laity and the ignorance in which the latter were being kept. Then there was the obvious geographical fact that Rome was a long way from the north of Europe, and the people resented the fact that they were obliged to pay their tithes to a distant, even foreign, power and have their lives so largely regulated from this source. Political and economic were much interwoven with religious factors, and the stage was set for rebellion when a sufficiently courageous and dynamic leader should emerge.

More important and more deep-seated than any of these practical matters was the strongly humanistic note of the Renaissance. Whether or not directly affiliated with a religious concern, it stressed the importance of the individual man. This emphasis, when taken in conjunction with the individual access of the soul to God and God's presence in the individual seeker which had been stressed in fourteenth-century mysticism, made fertile ground for the Reformation. The "Protestant principle," of which Paul Tillich was later to write so effectively, had come upon the scene. It has persisted to the present, even though at times obscured by concern for institutional structure and control in Protestant as well as Catholic circles. It is clearly at work today in the many demands for church renewal and for greater lay initiative in the management of the churches.

With the emergence of Protestantism, devotional writing as well as many other aspects of the religious life took a somewhat different turn. The break at this point was by no means complete or sharply defined. Protestants of today may still read and use with great profit the devotional and mystical writings of Roman Catholics who wrote both before and after the Reformation period—otherwise much of what has already been included in this book would be extraneous. Yet the mood and setting shifts from a largely monastic, or at least an intra-church, background to the Christian within the world. Its setting is chiefly man's need of forgiveness and grace, and of God's guidance and strengthening for the daily task, in all of one's manifold encounters. This becomes apparent if one compares, for example, *The Imitation of Christ* with almost any widely used Protestant devotional manual of today, such as John Baillie's *Diary of Private Prayer.*[1]

## 1. Luther and Calvin

I shall not attempt to say much about either the life story or the devotional writing of these two great leaders of the Reformation. The events of their connection with the Reformation are too well known to require it, and about their mystical writing there is not much to say. Both were devoted, courageous and extraordinarily able Christian men whose achievements and lasting influence merit all the tributes history has accorded them. Yet one may be a Christian without being a mystic.

Was Luther a mystic? A case may be made for either a yes or no answer, for in his earlier period of intense struggle to find a true relationship with God, he leans strongly in this direction. He seems clearly to have had the capacity for mystical experience. About Calvin the answer can be more decisive. He had not the temperament for it.

It will be recalled that Luther gave very high praise to the *Theologia Germanica* and published an edition of it in 1516, then believing it to have been written by John Tauler as an epitome of his sermons.[2] Calvin's strong repudiation of the book is equally symptomatic. Later, Luther's enthusiasm for the book somewhat cooled, as he found himself embroiled in the need to work out a theological and institutional form for the new Protestant movement. Yet he was definitely a man of prayer and deep personal piety. Scattered throughout his works, one finds some fine practical observations on prayer and worship. The reader will find these helpfully brought together from the various sources in Thomas S. Kepler's *Fellowship of the Saints*.[3] Yet though Luther's *Table Talk* comes nearest to laying bare his soul on such matters, he left no book that may properly be called mystical or devotional writing.

As for Calvin, he seems to have been born to be an interpreter and systematizer of Christian theology, a careful and painstaking expositor of the Scriptures, and a firm disciplinarian in what he believed to be for the glory of God and the right conduct of a Christian community. But if God ever designed him to be a mystic, the plan got mislaid along the way! This is not to say that it would have been impossible, for he was a sincere Christian with a powerful devotion to the God whom he sought to exalt and serve. Augustine, we have seen, was a mystic and at the same time a great theologian and ecclesiastical statesman, but such a combination does not appear very often and it seems to have passed Calvin by.[4]

If we cannot look to the beginnings of Protestantism for any great mystical or devotional writing, it emerged later, as we shall see presently. But, first, we must digress from the Protestant stream of development to look briefly at some great Roman Catholics of the Counter-Reformation. The three major figures we shall now mention left a profound influence and merit far more space than it is possible to give them. They are included here, not only because of their chronological sequence in the sixteenth century, but because their work was at least in part called forth by the impact of Protestantism and their deep desire to reform and extend the vitality of their own Catholic faith.

## 2. The Spanish Counter-Reformation

The cruelties of the Spanish Inquisition for the elimination of heresy and heretics is well known. We shall not deal with that, but with certain influential figures who adopted other methods for trying to establish and maintain the true Roman Catholic way. These are Ignatius Loyola, Teresa of Avila, and John of the Cross.

*a*) Ignatius of Loyola (1491-1556), son of a noble family in Northern Spain and for a time a page at the court of Ferdinand and Isabella, had a great ambition to pursue a military career. A wounded leg cut short this possibility, and while recovering he read devotional literature, especially the life of Christ and of the saints Dominic and Francis. After a considerable crisis of identity he resolved to devote his life to religion. This decision was confirmed in a year of solitude for reflection in a cave near Manresa.

Though Ignatius had now become a soldier of Christ, his military tastes and instincts had not left him. In 1534 he founded the Society of Jesus, which received the blessing of Pope Paul III in 1540. It had a strict spiritual and ecclesiastical discipline, with hierarchal orders of command, and its members took vows of absolute obedience to their superiors and to the pope. Its aim was to fight the battles of the Church against infidels and heretics, and by the end of the century it had become the advance guard of the Counter-Reformation through preaching, the confessional, its excellent schools, and its foreign missions. The Jesuit order was suppressed for political reasons toward the end of the eighteenth century and later restored. It has exerted great influence through the bearing of its missionary labors on colonization and its high standards of scholarship.

However, it is not the Jesuit order but the *Spiritual Exercises* designed to accompany it that entitles Ignatius to mention in a book of this type. Though basic to the Jesuit discipline and required of its members, this work of Ignatius antedates the Society of Jesus, having first appeared in 1522. It provides specifications for a four-week period of spiritual self-examination and dedication to Christ. In the first week one meditates upon his own sinfulness; in the second on the life of Christ and the call to serve him; in the third on Christ's passion and death; in the fourth on the risen and glorified Christ. The *Exercises* show much psychological acumen in their appeal to the imagination, their rhythms and repetitive sequences, an appeal to the bodily senses, and a biblical rootage made very personal in the life of the person who seriously engages in them.

How valuable are these to the Protestant? It depends on one's ability to adapt them to his circumstances, and not be deterred by occasional indications of Roman Catholic theology. Yet whatever their content, their *purpose* is wholly relevant to Protestant as well as Catholic, and very contemporary. The *Exercises* were designed as a manual for persons making a spiritual retreat, for the retreat movement is by no means as recent a development as it is often assumed to be. We have noted already the retreat centers of Jan van Ruysbroeck at Green Vale and the one founded by Rulman Merswin at Green Isle in the fourteenth century.

*b*) Teresa of Avila (1515-1582) was a remarkable woman. Though Ignatius organized his company of spiritual soldiers, Teresa gave new life to her order of Carmelite nuns by stressing both a discipline of the body and a need for deep inner communion with God. Her answer to the Protestant Reformation was the attempt to reform her church by reforming the religious within it. To do this she engaged in almost superhuman labors, and with a remarkable literary style wrote several books on the Christian life which still afford vital inspiration as we read them today.

At nineteen Teresa became a nun of the Carmelite order. After years of uneventful service in it, she resolved to bring it back to the more rigorous rules which had originally been established for it. Accordingly, she secured permission from the pope to found an order of Discalced, or Barefoot, nuns. This wearing of sandals instead of shoes was not an end in itself, but a symbol of the need of taking seriously the vows of poverty and renunciation of the comforts of the world. With the help of a younger contemporary, John of the Cross, this reformation in the form of a more exacting discipline was extended to friars as well as nuns.

This did not happen all at once. It took twenty years of labor, and much travel under incredible hardships and in spite of opposition from the church and occasional bouts of illness, to bring it to pass. Yet in the end, she had with John's assistance established seventeen monasteries for Discalced nuns and fifteen for the friars.

Much has been made by the critics of St. Teresa's unusual, if not psychotically abnormal, experiences. It is true, according to her own account, that she had visions, locutions, raptures, and ecstasies. On one occasion she had a vision of an angel who pierced her heart with a long golden dart tipped with fire, and when it was withdrawn she was left inflamed with a great love of God. At times she saw the Savior close beside her, and heard a voice saying, "Have no fear, daughter, for it is I, and I will not desert thee." Make what we will of such experiences, it is indisputable that her achievements manifest great spiritual strength and her writings contain many profound insights into the life of mystical devotion.

It is impossible here to do more than suggest the outlines of her mystical writings, of which the major works are her *Life, The Interior Castle,* and *The Way of Perfection.* She added little that was new but with a pungent literary style brought together many notes of the Catholic mystical tradition. This may be illustrated by her analogy of the soul as a garden to be watered—by drawing water laboriously from the well by hand, getting it more easily and abundantly by a windlass, having the ground saturated by a stream or brook, or seeing the Lord water it by showers of rain. These processes correspond to four degrees of mental prayer: a difficult beginning as the soul applies itself with effort to holy meditation; the prayer of Quiet, as the soul is led into peace by the Lord's presence; the Repose of the soul, in which union begins but the soul is still active; and the consummation of Union in which all the powers of the soul are absorbed in God with great joy.

Though Teresa faced and overcame great obstacles, she did not have to undergo overt persecution. Her younger co-worker did.

*c*) John of the Cross (1542-1591) affords a clear example of asceticism in the mystical tradition. An ascetic he was, but he was so much more that he holds a high place as one of the most creative of all the mystics.

Sponsored in his youth for the priesthood at one of the Jesuit schools, he chose instead to become a Carmelite friar. Even as a young man he practiced the austerities which were to continue throughout his life. He ate little, slept on a hollow board, wore the proverbial hair shirt. Meeting Teresa when he was twenty-five and she fifty-two, he readily consented to assist her in reform of the Carmelite order. Not only did he help her found the monasteries mentioned above, but as a man he was able to perform services then undreamed of as within the capacity of a woman. Thus he served as spiritual director, confessor, vicar, rector, prior, and counselor to a growing number of these houses.

But not all was smooth going. Nor were his austerities to be all of a voluntary origin. In a sharp dispute which arose between the Calced and Discalced Carmelites, he was seized and imprisoned in the monastery at Toledo. There he was confined in a small room only six feet by ten with scarcely any light, fed on bread and water, frequently scourged by the friars, and deprived of the Mass and the sacraments. This failed to break his spirit, and it was there that he wrote some of his greatest poetry. After eight and a half months he managed to climb over a wall and escape.

Both his reform activities and his mystical writing continued. He rose to considerable prominence in his order, only to be shorn of all power and "thrown into a corner like an old rag" by a rival's opposition and a whispering campaign.[5] He died in virtual exile soon after this rejection, but still with a gentle soul unembittered by the treatment accorded him.

John wrote four books of lasting importance: *The Ascent of Mount Carmel, The Dark Night of the Soul, The Spiritual Canticle,* and *The Living Flame of Love*. Together, they make an extensive survey of the contemplative life. The first two deal with ascetic mysticism; the last two describe the abounding and inflowing spiritual gifts of God. Together they cover the traditional mystical way of purgation, illumination, and union, but with considerable originality.

*The Ascent of Mount Carmel* accents the need of the individual to empty himself of self-love by denying himself any pleasure that leads to desire. Not only must he reject all natural entanglements, passing through "the night of sense," but also "the night of the spirit" lest one cultivate a gluttony of spiritual gifts. God will give us what we need without inordinate seeking. Thus far, the soul is active and takes the initiative in its self-preparation. But in *The Dark Night of the Soul* [6] the mood changes to a passivity not of one's own choosing. God seems to have forsaken one, and the soul suffers a painful period of dryness and the darkness of doubt and despair. This was a familiar experience to many of the mystics, but John was able to point the way forward better than most. For actually, he says, God is purifying the soul by this suffering, and leading the way to rise from a living death into new life.[7]

It is this brighter side of the mystical experience that John deals with in his last two books. *The Spiritual Canticle* sets forth the stages in the soul's progress toward union with God as love, spiritual betrothal, and spiritual marriage. Here we find recurring a familiar note from the Song of Songs, of which Bernard had made such extensive use. In *The Living Flame of Love* John attempts to describe what is admittedly indescribable, the union of the soul with God. Careful to avoid heresy, he does not claim that God and man become one in substance, but the soul "participates" in God so completely that one cannot discern where God's flame of love begins and his own ends.

This excursion into post-Reformation Catholic mysticism has, I trust, suggested the blend of tradition with reform that emerged in this period. But what of the ongoing stream of Protestant mystical piety?

## 3. Jacob Boehme

I must attempt, at least briefly, to say something about the beginnings of Protestant mysticism with a look at a man whose thought is very complex, his language unclear and full of allegorical symbolism, yet in some respects was ahead of his time.

In fact, I have heard Paul Tillich refer to him with great respect. We shall encounter him again later with William Law.

Jacob Boehme (1575-1624), known also as Behmen, was an unlearned shoemaker of Görlitz, Germany. He apparently read only the Bible and some works of the Swiss physician Paracelsus, yet from his own mind and what he regarded as God-given visions he produced an elaborate system which is a blend of theosophy, metaphysics, theology, and practical Christianity. He so shocked the orthodox that after his first book, *Aurora,* appeared, he was forbidden to write further. For some years he acceded; then he produced others which he felt the Lord had told him to write. For this he was banished, and he died in exile in Dresden.

A basic note in his system is the antithesis, or tension, in all things. "In Yes and No all things consist." This applies even to God, and it is "the dark nature of God," or the Abyss, which accounts for the evil in the world. But God himself is not evil. "Neither reason nor scripture will allow us to bring wrath into God Himself, as a temper of His mind, who is only infinite, unalterable, overflowing Love." [8] The visible world is a symbol of the invisible, and the light of the Spirit is in all things contending against the evil in nature and man.

Boehme laid great stress on the indwelling presence of Christ in the soul. This along with his denial of divine wrath put him at variance with orthodox views of atonement and imputed righteousness. "That man is no Christian who doth merely comfort himself with the suffering, death, and satisfaction of Christ, and doth impute it to himself as a gift of favour, remaining himself still a wild beast and unregenerate. . . . If this said sacrifice is to avail for me, it must be wrought *in* me." [9] Furthermore, Boehme was as sure as the author of the *Theologia Germanica* that all self-will must be stripped away. "In my own nothingness, I give glory to the Eternal Being, and will nothing of myself, that so God may will all in me, being unto me my God and all things." [10]

## 4. Lancelot Andrewes

Lancelot Andrewes (1555-1626) by any possible reckoning was a remarkable man. He was a very devout person and a linguistic genius, an ecclesiastical statesman of the highest order and a very humble soul, an author of many pages of sermonic, expository, and even argumentative prose. Yet he is best known for a small book of exquisite beauty, poetic resonance, and spiritual power, his *Private Devotions*. Written in Greek, they were designed for no eyes but his own.

To sum up the life story of this remarkable man, after an excellent education at Cambridge and various minor appointments, he served for three years as chaplain to Queen Elizabeth, then became canon of St. Paul's and dean of Westminster Abbey. After the accession of King James to the throne, he became his Privy Counselor. This led to his being asked by the King to become chairman of the committee responsible for translating the King James version of the Bible from Genesis through II Kings. This he was well equipped to do, for he was familiar with fifteen languages, which included Hebrew, though much of his own writing was done in Latin or Greek. He successively became Bishop of Chichester, of Ely, and of Winchester, though his biographer remarks of this advancement, "and all this on the account of his worth, without any ambitious suit or seeking of his own to qualify him for these preferments." [11]

*The Library of Anglo-Catholic Theology* contains several volumes of Andrewes' works. I have before me a collection of ninety-six of his sermons, each one designated as "preached before Queen Elizabeth" or "preached before the King's Majesty," with its date, place, and biblical text. There is also his *Pattern of Catechetical Doctrine* with various minor works in English and several in Latin. These I must leave aside to center attention on his *Private Devotions*. First published in 1675, the book has gone through numerous editions, of which I shall use the translation by John Henry Newman.[12]

The *Devotions* are arranged systematically, with preparatory instructions, and an order for matins and another for evening prayer, each with a meditation, confession and commendation. More extensive, however, are the prayers for each day of the week. These follow a fairly regular pattern of an introductory note of adoration, confession, a prayer for grace, profession of faith, intercession, praise, and thanksgiving. The book contains also prayers for individual occasions and needs.

Since the reader cannot appreciate the richness of these

prayers without some examples, I shall excerpt some passages from each of these moods as set forth for the first day of the week.[13]

*Introduction*

Through the tender mercies of our God
the day-spring from on high hath visited us.
Glory be to Thee, O Lord, glory to Thee.
Creator of the light,
and Enlightener of the world,—
of the visible light,
The Sun's ray, a flame of fire,
day and night,
evening and morning,—
of the light invisible,
the revelation of God,
writings of the Law,
oracles of Prophets,
music of Psalms,
instruction of Proverbs,
experience of Histories,—
light which never sets.

*1. Confession*

Merciful and pitiful Lord,
Long-suffering and full of pity,
I have sinned, Lord, I have sinned against Thee;
O me, wretched that I am,
I have sinned, Lord, against Thee
much and grievously,
in attending on vanities and lies.
I conceal nothing:
I make no excuses.
I give Thee glory, O Lord, this day,
I denounce against myself my sins;
Truly I have sinned before the Lord,
and thus and thus have I done.

2. *Prayer for grace*

Vouchsafe to me, to worship Thee and serve Thee
1. in truth of spirit,
2. in reverence of body,
3. in blessing of lips,
4. in private and in public;
5. to pay honour to them that have the rule over me,
by obedience and submission,
to shew affection to my own
by carefulness and providence;

6. to overcome evil with good;
7. to possess my vessel in sanctification and honour;
8. to have my converse without covetousness,
content with what I have;
9. to speak the truth in love;
10. to be desirous not to lust,
not to lust passionately,
not to go after lusts.

3. *Profession*

I believe, O Lord;
help Thou mine unbelief,
and vouchsafe to me
to love the Father for His fatherly love,
to reverence the Almighty for His power,
as a faithful Creator, to commit my soul to Him
in well doing;
vouchsafe to me to partake
from Jesus of salvation,
from Christ of anointing,
from the Only-begotten of adoption;
to worship the Lord
for His conception in faith,
for His birth in humility,
for His sufferings in patience and hatred of sin;
for His cross to crucify beginnings,
for His death to mortify the flesh,
for His burial to bury evil thoughts in good works,
for His descent to meditate upon hell,
for His resurrection upon newness of life,
for His ascension, to mind things above,
for His sitting on high, to mind the good things on
His right,
for His return, to fear His second appearance,
for judgment, to judge myself ere I be judged.
From the Spirit
vouchsafe me the breath of salutary grace.

4. *Intercession*

Remember, Lord,
infants, children, the grown, the young,
the middle aged, the old,
hungry, thirsty, naked, sick,
prisoners, foreigners, friendless, unburied,
all in extreme age and weakness,
possessed with devils, and tempted to suicide,
troubled by unclean spirits,
the hopeless, the sick in soul or body, the weak-hearted,

all in prison and chains, all under sentence of death;
orphans, widows, foreigners, travellers, voyagers,
women with child, women who give suck,
all in bitter servitude, or mines, or galleys,
or in loneliness.

5. *Praise*

Up with our hearts;
We lift them to the Lord.
O how very meet, and right, and fitting, and due,
in all, and for all,
at all times, places, manners,
in every season, every spot,
everywhere, always, altogether,
to remember Thee, to worship Thee,
to confess to Thee, to praise Thee,
to bless Thee, to hymn Thee,
to give thanks to Thee,
Maker, nourisher, guardian, governor,
preserver, worker, perfecter of all,
Lord and Father,
King and God,
fountain of life and immortality,
treasure of everlasting goods.

These excerpts, each of which stands in a more extended context, are perhaps enough to suggest the tenor of the *Devotions*. Not all of the diction is contemporary, but the thoughts and aspirations expressed are timeless.

## 5. George Fox

We shall now bypass a considerable period to come to George Fox (1624-1691) who was born two years before Andrewes died. It would be difficult to find two Protestant Christians more unlike than they, and it may be of interest to view them in juxtaposition.

George Fox, the son of a weaver of Fenny Drayton, raised in a conventionally moral home but with only a minimal education, was a "nobody" from the standpoint of any normal expectations. Yet he turned out to be one of the major religious geniuses of England whose influence is still widely and creatively felt in the Society of Friends, of which he was the founder. His *Journal*, his only major piece of writing, is not only a fascinating autobiography but a devotional classic.

Fox seems to have been a somewhat serious-minded child, but his real story begins at the age of nineteen, when he became greatly disturbed by being asked to drink at a fair by two professing Christians. To discover that those professing Christ (whom he usually refers to in the book as "professors") did not always live as they spoke precipitated in him an emotional shock. In a deep emotional crisis he left his family to become for a time a solitary wanderer, seeking light from the Scriptures and from "priests and preachers," who failed to give him any help. He puts it in these words:

> I saw that there was none among them all that could speak to my condition. And when all my hopes in them and in all men were gone, so that I had nothing outwardly to help me, nor could I tell what to do; then, oh, then, I heard a voice which said, "There is one, even Christ Jesus, that can speak to thy condition"; and when I heard it my heart did leap for joy . . . and this I knew experimentally.[14]

This was the turning-point in Fox's life. So filled was he with a new faith that he began to witness to any who would listen. He recounts thereafter various visions, chiefly of his own sinfulness and the Lord's refining fire. Then in perplexity over the eternal problem of the evil in men's hearts, including his own, an illumination came to him which is one of the finest passages in the *Journal* and which explains much of his later power.

> I cried to the Lord, saying, "Why should I be thus, seeing I was never addicted to commit those evils?" and the Lord answered that it was needful I should have a sense of all conditions, and in this I saw the infinite love of God. I saw also that there was an ocean of darkness and death, but an infinite ocean of light and love which flowed over the ocean of darkness. In that also I saw the infinite love of God; and I had great openings.[15]

Fox continued to have his "great openings," and to witness in the power of the Holy Spirit, which he saw as the Inner Light, to his newfound faith. The churches of his day he refers to as "steeple-houses," and he was seldom welcome in them. Instead he spoke to small groups, then as they grew, to larger assemblies wherever they came together to hear him. These groups became the nucleus of the Society of Friends. Sometimes in disparagement they were called Quakers because of the great religious feeling that was experienced and manifest through the power of the Spirit.

These groups of Friends, banded together as Christ's followers without creed or sacrament but led by the Inner Light, had only a minor amount of visible organization, but powerful convictions. Under Fox's leadership and example, they renounced war and every form of violence. When Fox was asked if he would take up arms for the Commonwealth against Charles Stuart, he replied "that I lived in the virtue of that life and power that took away the occasion of all wars." They believed in the equality of all persons, women as well as men. They had no officially employed clergymen, each being free to speak, testify, or pray in meeting as the Spirit moved, but some were looked to as leaders and there were women preachers as well as males. This sense of human equality led them to refuse to do homage to dignitaries. They aimed to speak the truth at all times, but would take no oaths.

Furthermore, these people felt the calling of the Lord to minister to human suffering wherever it was to be found. They defended the rights of the poor, attempted to reform the prisons, demanded justice for the oppressed. A century later when slavery became an acute issue in America, Fox's successor John Woolman was in the forefront of the anti-slavery movement.

In 1671-73 Fox visited America, where he traveled extensively in New England and along the Eastern seaboard, establishing there numerous groups of the Society of Friends, to some of whom William Penn was later to come as the governor of Pennsylvania. However, the greater part of Fox's life was given to establishing and ministering to such groups in England. In this he was opposed by John Bunyan, who believed the Quakers made too much of the Inner Light and not enough of the Scriptures. The principal opposition, however, came from the Church of England, which found such an unconventional form of Protestantism very distasteful. Not only Fox himself but his followers were repeatedly imprisoned, and he endured a long series of such confinements under conditions which would have broken the spirit of a less resolute person.

This is not to imply perfection in Fox's character. Rufus Jones wishes that he had not taken so much satisfaction in the "judgments" which overtook many of the persons who persecuted him.

Yet more than once he won the love and appreciation of his judges and his jailers. On the whole, his life exemplified these words of advice which he gave to his followers:

> Be patterns, be examples in all countries, places, islands, nations, wherever you come, that your carriage and life may preach among all sorts of people, and to them; then you will come to walk cheerfully over the world, answering that of God in every one.[16]

The Quakers of today, still a minority group but respected throughout the world, may well claim George Fox as their progenitor.

## 6. William Law

With some reluctance I must pass by John Bunyan, who had his own merits and achievements even if he did not like the Quakers. But both his life story and his *Pilgrim's Progress*—and to a less extent his *Grace Abounding,* are too familiar to need much space, and this book is already becoming too long. So let us move now to the eighteenth century and make the acquaintance of William Law.

William Law (1686-1761) is important for a number of reasons. His book *A Serious Call to a Devout and Holy Life* is worth reading for its own sake. Furthermore, he had considerable influence on John Wesley, and stirred both Samuel Johnson and John Henry Newman to serious thoughts about their religion. Thus, his brand of evangelical Protestant piety cast a long shadow into the future.

By contrast with most of the others we have considered, William Law's life was uneventful. He neither founded a new religious order, nor was a great preacher or high ecclesiastic or a teacher of renown. He was, however, an independent spirit, a Christian with a conscience, and a writer whose work lived after him.

He was born in the village of King's Cliffe in Northhamptonshire, the son of a prosperous merchant, and grew up in a religious home. In 1711 he bacame a fellow of Emmanuel College, Cambridge, and was ordained as a deacon in the Anglican Church. But he was a Puritan at heart. On the accession of George I to the throne in 1714, Law refused to swear allegiance to the House of Hanover. As a non-juror, this ended his fellowship at Cambridge and any chance of ecclesiastical advancement.

In 1726 he became the tutor of Edward Gibbon, the father of the famous historian of that name, and returned with him to Emmanuel College. There he began his writing career, and from then on his destinies were linked with the Gibbon family. When the elder Gibbon died in 1739, Law returned to his ancestral home at King's Cliffe. There he lived quietly until his death, most of these years with a Mrs. Hutcheson and Miss Hester Gibbon, the sister of his former pupil. The three were active in numerous works of charity and devotion.

Law's most lasting writings were produced in his second Cambridge period, *Christian Perfection* in 1726 and *A Serious Call* (as we shall now refer to it) in 1728. It was during this period also, though later than the writing of these books, that he developed strongly mystical insights, mainly from the reading of Eckhart, Tauler, and Jacob Boehme. In 1740 he published *An Appeal to All That Doubt* and somewhat later *The Way of Divine Love* and *The Spirit of Prayer*.

It is difficult to summarize these works, for their primary importance lies not in glowing passages but in a permeating sense of the need of a religious revival in what had become the conventional religiosity of England. Many years before Kiekegaard, he was as eager to "put Christianity back into Christendom." Though an older contemporary of Wesley, he shared Wesley's concern and helped to instill it in him. While this note appears in all his writing, it is the *Serious Call* that has become its most classic expression.

Law was very methodical in his prayer life. The devotional pattern which forms the main structure of the *Serious Call* runs like this:

Upon rising *early*—Praise, adoration and thanksgiving
At nine o'clock—Prayer for humility
At twelve o'clock—Prayer of universal love and intercession
At three o'clock—Prayer of resignation and doing the will of God
At six o'clock—Prayer of self-examination, confession and repentance
At bed-time—Thoughts upon death and commitment to God

This may well have been the regimen followed in the King's

Cliffe household. But should it sound perfunctory, the greater part of the *Serious Call* consists of reflection upon these themes, with the suggestion of fruitful disciplines and emphasis on the centrality of these elements in the life of the Christian.

Law was a mystic but a very practical one, believing that inner communion with God must be accompanied by deeds of service to any in need. Accordingly, he established a school for girls in his home town, and later with his two associates a similar school for boys and a hospital for widows. It is said that every day he could be seen distributing the milk from their four cows to the neighbors in need. These are but a few of their benevolent acts.

Law wrote with keen psychological discernment, spiced not only with shrewd observations but with humor. Interspersed with suggestions for the devotional needs of the Christian one finds page after page of very readable incidents, probably imaginary but in the nature of modern parables, about persons who defeat their own aspirations for inner peace and happiness by silly desires and sillier actions. The reader will find many of these excerpted by Thomas Kepler in *The Fellowship of the Saints,* the concluding passage ending with these sage words:

> How ignorant, therefore, are they of the nature of religion, of the nature of man, and the nature of God, who think a life of strict piety and devotion to God to be a dull uncomfortable state; when it is so plain and certain that there is neither comfort nor joy to be found in anything else! [17]

William Law and John Wesley had so much in common that one would like to report that they remained friends and coworkers all their days. They both believed in Christian perfection as growth in grace and in the love and service of God; both believed in the union of faith with works. Both attached major importance to the disciplines of prayer (though Wesley was too busy for such an exactly timed regimen); and most important of all, they both yearned with all their souls for the revitalization of the religion of England. Yet one must report that their friendship cooled. After Law became a mystic, and especially after he fell under the spell of Boehme, Wesley could no longer approve his theology, and each went his own way. Wesley in his *Journal* disparages some of Law's later writings as warmly as he had praised the earlier. Yet there seems to be little question that Law left a permanent stamp on Wesley's thought, and through him on his spiritual descendants.

## 7. Were the Wesleys Mystics?

A final question needs to be raised before the conclusion of the chapter. Were the Wesleys, John and Charles, in their own way mystics even if not in the pattern of their predecessors? We have seen that mysticism took many forms—what about these men?

About Charles Wesley, my answer would be in the affirmative. One does not write six thousand hymns which radiate the spirit of ebullient joy in the Lord and move us still after two hundred years with a sense of the presence of God, and not have an unusual sense of the immediacy of the divine Spirit. I do not know whether Charles Wesley would have wished to be called a mystical genius but the fruits of his labors justify this designation.

As for John Wesley, I doubt that this term is applicable. This is not to disparage his monumental labors for the salvation of souls and the effort to "spread Scriptural holiness over the land." But as has been indicated repeatedly, not every Christian, not even every great Christian, is a mystic.

Why, then, deny him this designation? One indication may lie in his dispute with William Law over Boehme. We find in his *Journal:* "I read over Mr. Law's book on the New Birth: philosophical, speculative, precarious; Behemenish, void and vain." And again:

> I read Mr. Law on the Spirit of Prayer. There are many masterly strokes therein, and the whole is lively and entertaining; but it is another Gospel: for if God was never angry (as this Tract asserts) He could never be reconciled; and consequently the whole Christian doctrine of Reconciliation by Christ falls to the ground at once. An excellent method of converting Deists! By giving up the very essence of Christianity.[18]

This is clearly a protest against Law's theology. But it is more —a protest against Law's mysticism, for if one felt in sympathy with it he would find much more in *The Spirit of Prayer* than what might be designated as "lively and entertaining." In his earlier years Wesley was much attracted to Jeremy Taylor's *Rules and Exercises of Holy Living and Holy Dying* and to *The Imitation of Christ*. But whatever mystical tendencies this may indicate were later disavowed. In a letter to his brother Samuel in 1736 he states that the rock on which he had nearest made shipwreck of the faith was the writings of the mystics. In 1741 an entry in his Journal indicates strong disapproval of Luther's commentary on Galatians, and he says of him that "he is deeply tinctured with mysticism throughout, and hence often dangerously wrong." [19]

Neither Wesley's activist temperament nor his theology was congenial to his understanding of mysticism. But there was also a historical reason for his protests. A movement known as Quietism had emerged which merits much more attention than can here be given to it. After the three great Roman Catholic mystics of the Counter-Reformation period discussed earlier in this chapter had passed from the scene, a fourth Spanish mystic emerged, Miguel Molinos (1640-1697). His *Spiritual Guide* pointed the way to inner peace through a quiet waiting before God and reliance on the inward authority of the Spirit, not unlike the Society of Friends. This aroused a furor among the church authorities, who branded his Quietism a dangerous heresy. A little later the same fate befell the French Madame Guyon (1648-1717). While Wesley expressed sympathy for her in the treatment that had been accorded Madame Guyon, he had no love for Quietism. It was too foreign to his activist spirit, and seemed a betrayal of much that he felt vital to Christian faith.

This opposition lingers today, in the assumption that the mystics do nothing but sit or kneel in prayer while other Christians do the work of the world in the service of God and humanity. I hope that enough has been said in this book to dispel this widely held false notion. Yet so persistent is it that I hope to deal with it, head-on, in the next chapter by citing some contemporary activists who were at the same time steeped in a mysticism from which they drew their deepest incentives.

# VII

# Some Twentieth-century Mystics

During the earlier chapters of this book I have attempted to give a brief interpretation of some important figures in Christian history, both Roman Catholic and Protestant, who are distinguished for their mystical insights or for the production of lasting devotional classics. As I explained earlier, this could not possibly be a complete compendium. There are too many of them to treat even briefly without running the book far out of bounds. I have also tried to quote enough from most of these authors to give something of the flavor of their writing without any pretense at a complete anthology.

The purpose of this chapter is somewhat different. Many people seem to think of mystics as people who lived far away and long ago, and had little connection if any with important events in the world. I hope to indicate by citing a number of twentieth-century persons, well-known names to most readers of this book, that such isolation from reality is far from being the case. Those I have selected are best known for other achievements, but their incentives stemmed from a deeply mystical base. None of these are now living, yet in a real sense they are our contemporaries.

## 1. Frank C. Laubach

Frank Laubach (1884-1970) has often been called "an apostle to the illiterates." Nobody knows the exact number of persons who have been taught to read through his methods and incentive, but it is certainly well over sixty million persons in over three hundred languages and dialects in more than one hundred countries of the world. With such new literacy has come emancipation from bondage, better modes of living, a fuller sense of personhood for innumerable persons. One government after another has invited Dr. Laubach to bring his teaching methods

and personnel to their countries, and the succession of medals and high honors that he has received for this service would have completely turned the head of a less humble person.

The main basis of the Laubach method consists in two relatively simple but important steps. The first is the preparation of a pictorial chart that by combining the picture of a familiar object, the word that designates it, and its principal sound in printed form soon teaches the learner to recognize the word and use it in other related combinations. With the elation of now being able to read even a little comes the second step—the "each one, teach one" method by which one now goes and teaches his neighbor what he has learned. Thus, the process multiplies and has proved remarkably successful. Furthermore, the simple reading matter produced for new literates has done much to teach better sanitation and prevention of disease, better methods of agriculture, and much else of a socially beneficial nature. While Dr. Laubach has written a number of books in this field as well as others of a religious nature, the one which most fully shows both the needs and the possibilities of instruction in literacy for vast numbers of people is *The Silent Billion Speak.*[1]

But what lies back of all this achievement by one unpretentious, humble man?

After an excellent education at Princeton University and Union Theological Seminary, some years of social work in New York City, and a Ph.D. from Columbia University, Dr. Laubach in 1915 went with his wife to the Philippines as a missionary. There he helped to found and for a time served as a member of the faculty of Union Theological Seminary in Manila, an excellent institution in which I myself taught for a time much later, in 1957. But on the island of Mindanao lived some half-million Moslem Moros, a wild and backward people who looked upon the Christian Filipinos as their natural enemies. To this group Dr. Laubach asked to be transferred.

Those first weeks in Mindanao were very difficult ones, for on account of health factors his wife and young son had stayed in Dumaguete in a safer location. He was very lonely, and discouraged at his failure to make any headway with the Moros. Then on a memorable night as he watched the sun set over Lake Lanao from Signal Hill, he had a mystical experience which

changed the tenor of his life. One aspect of it was that, as he tells it, he realized that he did not "really love those Moros. In that terrible, wonderful hour on Signal Hill I became color-blind. Ever since, I have been partial to tan—the more tan the better. Every missionary goes through some such experience as that—or comes home defeated." [2] He came alive with a great love for the Moros.

The other aspect of his new experience was his realization that he must try to think of God at every moment, and put his trust and his life completely in the hands of God. The letters which he wrote in the ensuing months have been compiled in a small book entitled *Letters by a Modern Mystic*.[3] It is a moving account of his growth in what Brother Lawrence three centuries earlier had called "The Practice of the Presence of God." It is a classic among descriptions of personal experiences in mystical communion, sometimes joyously advancing, sometimes slipping a bit in one's resolution, but going forward again undaunted.

There is not space to quote at length from this remarkable witness, but two or three citations will indicate its mystical, yet very practical savor.

> We used to sing a song in the church at Benton [his home town in Pennsylvania] which I liked, but which I never really practiced until now. It runs:
>
> Moment by moment I'm kept in His love;
> Moment by moment, I've life from above;
> Looking to Jesus till glory doth shine;
> Moment by moment, O Lord, I am thine.
>
> It is exactly that "moment by moment," every waking moment, surrender, responsiveness, obedience, sensitiveness, pliability, "lost in His love," that I now have the mind-bent to explore with all my might. It means two burning passions: First, to be like Jesus. Second, to respond to God as a violin responds to the bow of the master.[4]

Quite naturally, this new sense of the divine Presence made a difference in Dr. Laubach's work, though no one save God could yet foresee what a vast difference it was to make in his usefulness in the years to come. In a letter written some six weeks later we find him witnessing to the change that had come about in his immediate relations with the Moros:

> For the first time in my life I know what I must do off in lonesome Lanao. I know why God left this aching void, for himself to fill. . . .

I must confront these Moros with a divine love which will speak Christ to them though I never use his name. They must see God in me, and I *must* see God in them. Not to change the name of their religion, but to take their hand and say, "Come, let us look for God." [5]

Two months after he had begun his strenuous effort to keep God continually in his thought, he gives this self-analysis which sounds much like the witness of St. Teresa and some of the other great mystics:

This concentration upon God is *strenuous,* but everything else has ceased to be so. I think more clearly, I forget less frequently. Things which I did with a strain before, I now do easily and with no effort whatever. I worry about nothing, and lose no sleep. I walk on air a good part of the time. Even the mirror reveals a new light in my eyes and face. I no longer feel in a hurry about anything. Everything goes right. Each minute I meet calmly as though it were not important. Nothing can go wrong excepting one thing. That is that God *may slip from my mind* if I do not keep on my guard. If He is there, the universe is with me. My task is simple and clear.[6]

Those of us who knew Dr. Laubach in his later years can testify that this was no passing phase. He always seemed to be completely calm and self-possessed and never in a hurry, yet his many engagements were met apparently without effort whether in America or in his many travels around the world. I asked him once whether it was psychologically possible to think of God at every minute and still get any work done in the business at hand. His answer was engagingly simple. He said, "It is perfectly possible to think of more than one matter at the same time. At this moment I am thinking of God, of you, of what we are talking about, and of what we have to do when I speak to your students this evening." This seemed incontrovertible.

Let no one think of Frank Laubach and say that a mystical communion with God makes no difference to the world! This is how he speaks of his illiterates, "The most bruised people on this planet, the naked, the hungry, the fallen among thieves, the sick, the imprisoned in mind and soul, are the twelve hundred million illiterates, three-fifths of the human race. . . . More than half the human race is hungry, driven, diseased, afraid of educated men in this world and of demons in the next." [7] And he ministered to them.

## 2. Toyohiko Kagawa

Several years ago it used to be said that whatever the disorders of that time, we were living in a period which had produced three great saints—Gandhi in India, Schweitzer in Africa, and Kagawa in Japan. Unquestionably all three were great, good men, and even if their frequent citation in inspirational addresses became a bit too familiar for freshness, they deserved the tributes paid them. I shall not attempt to judge which was the greatest, for they lived in different situations, made different contributions, and—let us admit it—had some different points of weakness as well as of strength.

My reason for selecting Kagawa for special mention is simply that he fits better the purposes of this book. The other two were men of great dedication and great faith—the one Hindu and the other Christian—but the mystical-devotional element seems to me to stand out less clearly in their lives than in Kagawa's.

Toyohiko Kagawa (1888-1960) had an unhappy childhood. His father was a prominent person, secretary of the Privy Council to the Emperor, but the boy was the son of a concubine and thus held to be of inferior status. Both parents died when he was four, and he was brought up in loneliness and rejection. It was only when in adolescence two missionaries came into his life that he learned to know love. Through them he found Christ, and this brought meaning and purpose to his life.

This led to a decision to devote his life to the poor, whereupon his uncle, the head of the family, disinherited him. Yet he persisted, entering the Presbyterian College of Tokyo and later the theological seminary of Kobe in preparation for the Christian ministry.

Yet even before his ordination, his next move was into the Shinkawa slums.

Hardened as we are to the conditions in the urban ghettoes of America, the Shinkawa slums of that day seem almost indescribable. I shall let one of Kagawa's biographers describe them:

> At that time there were in this section, known as the Shinkawa, some twenty thousand outcasts, paupers, criminals, beggars, prostitutes, and defectives, who lived like homeless dogs in human kennels of filth and vermin and disease. Policemen feared to visit this district unless they went in groups. Often a single house, not more than six feet square, would accomodate a family of five, or two families of nine to ten persons.

A community kitchen, a water hydrant, and a common toilet of unspeakable filth often served the needs of a score of families. The district swarmed with scrofulous, undernourished children, and the infantile mortality rate often reached the staggering height of over 500 in 1,000.[8]

Into this horrible mess, while still completing his seminary studies, the young Kagawa moved. His room, about six feet square, he shared with one unfortunate person after another, some with communicable diseases. It was here that he contracted the trachoma which followed him the rest of his life. Here he washed their infected clothing, taught classes in reading and writing, and even adopted and nursed back to life a starving baby girl. Meanwhile he carried on his own studies at the seminary and did considerable writing, including poetry which has been preserved in *Songs from the Slums*.

The way then opened for Kagawa to study for two years in America at Princeton Theological Seminary. This was a turning-point in his career, for thereafter he was known in the dual capacity of religious leader and organizer of labor unions and many kinds of consumer cooperatives. He was expecially concerned not only with Japan's rapidly growing body of industrial workers but with the tenant farmers of the overpopulated arable land areas who were adding to the congestion in the urban slums. At the International Missionary Conference of 1938, I heard him express his whole socio-religious philosophy in one trenchant sentence, "We must baptize our bread and butter!"

But what of Dr. Kagawa's mysticism? We know less of it than of Dr. Laubach's, but for many years in the midst of his many labors he spent an hour of each day, often in the middle of the night, in personal communion with God. In fact, it was from a description by him of this communion which was given in a conversation that I derived the title of a poem of mine, "I listen to the agony of God." Clear evidence, however, of his mystical spirit is found in his writing. I shall quote two of my favorites from the *Songs of the Slums* because I believe they speak not only for Kagawa and Japan but for ourselves—each of us—in our own beloved country.

Discovery

I cannot invent
New things,

Like the airships  
Which sail  
On silvery wings;  
But today  
A wonderful thought  
In the dawn was given,  
And the stripes on my robe,  
Shining from wear,  
Were suddenly fair,  
Bright with a light  
Falling from Heaven—  
Gold, and silver, and bronze  
Lights from the windows of Heaven.

And the thought  
Was this:  
That a secret plan  
Is hid in my hand;  
That my hand is big,  
Big,  
Because of this plan.

That God,  
Who dwells in my hand,  
Knows this secret plan  
Of the things He will do for the world  
Using my hand! [9]

In the spring of 1957 it was my privilege with a number of friends to visit Dr. and Mrs. Kagawa in their simple home on the outskirts of Tokyo, next to an equally simple church and near a bevy of kindergartners at play. It was a better residence, I am sure, than the Shinkawa slums, but I would guess it to be plainer than anything occupied by most of the readers of this book! Yet how much God has been able to do with this one man's hands!

The other poem reflects the burden, both for one's self and one's country, and the only source of strength by which to go forward. It is especially appropriate both to our land and to that of its author, which we may rejoice are now at peace with each other after years of bitter struggle.

The Burden

Take Thou the burden, Lord;  
I am exhausted with this heavy load.

My tired hands tremble,
And I stumble, stumble
Along the way.
Oh, lead with Thine unfailing arm
Again today.

Unless Thou lead me, Lord,
The road I journey on is all too hard.
Through trust in Thee alone
Can I go on.

Yet not for self alone
Thus do I groan;
My people's sorrows are the load I bear.
Lord, hear my prayer—

May Thy strong hand
Strike off all chains
That load my well-loved land.
God, draw her close to Thee! [10]

Dr. Kagawa wrote at least one novel, *A Grain of Wheat,* besides these poems and various incidental articles, but it is this little volume of poems that is most likely to live. His cooperatives have been regarded by some economists as inadequate for an economy rooted in heavy industry, and less is heard of them than formerly. Yet some of them survive—we visited a cooperative grocery near his home—and for their time and place they were of enormous value in reducing the cost of food, clothing, money-lending, and many other needs of the Japanese poor. So once more we may say that a humble, God-centered man affected the course of history.

We shall look now at a saintly man and mystic who was nearly contemporary in his early years with the two whom we have now noted, though his death came earlier and in his lifetime he was little known in the United States.

## 3. Pierre Teilhard de Chardin

Pierre Teilhard de Chardin (1881-1955) was a dedicated priest, a prophet of an emerging new world, a faithful member of the Jesuit order, a world-famous geologist and paleontologist, a philosopher, and withal a poet and a Christian mystic. Because he was ahead of his time in seeing the possibility and the necessity of bringing science and the Christian faith into a mutually supporting, philosophically and theologically grounded relationship, most of his books were banned by the Roman Catholic Church and were little generally known until after his death in virtual exile in New York in 1955.

Pierre Teilhard de Chardin, whom we shall hereafter refer to simply as Teilhard, was the fourth child among eleven in a devout, close-knit, well-to-do French family. He was born at Sarcenat, though the family had a number of chateaux to which they went at various seasons of the year. His mother was a deeply religious woman, and writing of her toward the end of his life he says of her, "A spark had to fall upon me, to make the fire blaze out. And, without any doubt, it was through my mother that it came upon me, sprung from the stream of Christian mysticism, to light up and kindle by childish soul." [11] A more different home background from that of Kagawa could hardly be imagined!

At eighteen he entered the Jesuit novitiate, and these were his principal studies for several years. Yet he had an insatiable interest in rocks, and at twenty-one took his first geological field trip to Jersey. This was to be followed later by many others which made him an outstanding paleontologist, but not immediately. He did his required three years of Jesuit teaching in a college in Cairo. He continued to study theology interspersed with geological field trips and was ordained a priest. At the outbreak of the First World War he was called up for service in the medical corps as a stretcher-bearer, and received the Croix de Guerre. At the war's end he completed his studies for a doctorate in geology.

It might appear from this combination of geological with theological interests that he did not know his own mind and was being pulled in opposite directions. Actually, the conviction was taking shape in his mind that since the material and spiritual worlds are both God's handiwork and belong to God, there should be no such separation between them as had often been assumed. To bring together in a closer synthesis the physical realm and the world of the spirit, with man as the bond of connection between the two, was henceforth to be his major concern.

The next great event was a trip to China with a group of geologists and paleontologists, during which an important discovery was made, an uncrushed adult Sinanthropus skull, the first of its kind to be located. This was followed by numerous other expeditions to China and to Africa. It was during these trips that he wrote *The Phenomenon of Man,*[12] often considered to be his most important book, which was proscribed by his Church because of its clear affirmation of the long history of man through the evolutionary process. While Teilhard was distressed at this rejection, as a loyal Jesuit he accepted it and continued to write for his own satisfaction and because he felt led to do so.

Among other books of major importance written by Teilhard are *The Future of Man,*[13] *The Making of a Mind,*[14] *Letters from a Traveler,*[15] *The Divine Milieu,*[16] and *Hymn of the Universe.*[17] His church permitted some other scientific treatises to be published, but it is upon those of a philosophical or mystical nature that his fame chiefly rests.

It would obviously be impossible to summarize in a paragraph or two Teilhard's architectonic system. Yet the gist of it may be hinted at. It centers in a Christian evolutionary world view, whereby the cosmos progresses continually, though not without opposition, toward an ultimate "Omega point." The Omega point is the unity toward which all levels of existence converge, through the personal design of God the Creator Spirit. The Omega point is also epitomized in the universal Christ, for "He is before all things, and in him all things hold together" (Colossians 1:17). But what of man in this onward-moving process? The highest element in the cosmos is the Noosphere, the realm of mind and spirit, and in this, man in spite of all his sinfulness and incompleteness stands supreme. Man represents the highest level of consciousness in the total cosmic system, though God is the ultimate arbiter of human destiny. Teilhard therefore refuses to despair in spite of the evil of the times, for his hope is grounded in the Incarnation and the ultimate response of men to the divine love which the Incarnation makes concrete and universal as the focus of salvation.

This is clearly a form of process theology, not grounded primarily on Whitehead as much of it is today, but based on a synthesis of Teilhard's lifelong scientific studies with a clear conviction that "Christ is all and in all." He felt the presence and activity of God to be basic to man's effort in the forward movement toward the Omega point, and this gave to his entire life, in the midst of his innumerable diggings and scientific achievements, a deeply religious foundation.

This note recurs repeatedly in his writings. Only one or two must suffice. As he settled down in the midst of an expedition in Tientsin in 1926 to write *The Divine Milieu,* he wrote to a friend, "I have settled down to the little book I plan. I want to write it slowly, quietly—living it and meditating on it like a prayer." [18] The book reveals this quality. All of his writings radiate the spirit of a deep devotion to the Lord of the universe.

*The Hymn of the Universe* is the most distinctly mystical of Teilhard's books. Here he tells of a vision in a chapel which has the marks of a mystical illumination such as most scientists would hesitate to narrate, and the book radiates with a poetic beauty in the author's adoration and praise to the Lord of the universe. But in *The Divine Milieu* he deals in more formal language with the difference between true and false mysticism.

> In the general rhythm of Christian life, development and renunciation, attachment and detachment, are not mutually exclusive. . . . From this "dynamic" point of view the opposition so often stressed between asceticism and mysticism disappears. . . . Of course as God takes possession of man, the creature finally becomes passive (because it finds itself newly created in the divine union). But that passivity presupposes a subject that reacts and an active phase. The fire of heaven must come down on something: otherwise there would be nothing consumed and nothing consummated.[19]

Elsewhere the author makes it unmistakably clear that no vague sense of the presence of the resurrected Christ, apart from the Incarnate Christ of the gospel story, will suffice for true mysticism. "The mystical Christ, the universal Christ of St. Paul, has neither meaning nor value in our eyes except as an expansion of the Christ who was born of Mary and who died on the cross." [20] To recognize this, he says, is the antidote to visionaries and the "illuminati" who want to have their divine illuminations without their being grounded in the firm realities of the world we live in.

Teilhard seems to be saying here what I have tried to indicate repeatedly—that mystical devotion in its best sense is found *within* and not *in dissociation from* the total stream of human events. It may appear in visions, illuminations, and even in a transitory but rapturous sense of union with deity, and still be mysticism. But when it breaks radically with the concrete world of reality, suspect it! In any case, the surest proof of its reality is what ensues in the day-by-day living of the individual within his total universe.

The last four years of Teilhard's life were spent, for the most part, either in South Africa on further paleontology expeditions to sites on which he had already made important discoveries or in the United States, where he had many friends and felt somewhat more welcome than in his native France. Amid these travels he continued to write as his time permitted, eagerly seeking to complete *Le Christique,* his spiritual testament. He died on Easter Sunday in 1955, in New York. Perhaps I cannot better conclude this brief sketch of a great man and mystic than by quoting what he wrote in March of that year for this, his final work:

> Everywhere on earth, at this moment, within the new spiritual atmosphere created by the appearance of the idea of evolution, there float—in a state of extreme mutual sensitivity—the two essential components of the Ultra-human, love of God and faith in the world. Everywhere these two components are "in the air": generally, however, they are not strong enough, *both at the same time,* to combine with one another *in one and the same subject.* In me, by pure chance (temperament, education, environment) the proportion of each happens to be favourable, and they fuse together spontaneously. The fusion of the two is still not strong enough to spread explosively, but even so it is enough to show that such an explosion is possible and that, *sooner or later the chain-reaction will get under way.*
>
> It is one more proof that if the truth appears once, in a single mind, that is enough to ensure that nothing can ever prevent it from spreading to everything and setting it ablaze.[21]

And so it remains today, that the two components most needed for our times are love of God and faith in the world.

## 4. Dag Hammarskjöld

We have now looked at something of the life story and religious experience of three mystics of the twentieth century who to an unusual degree did combine the love of God with faith in the world, and as a result contributed much to the world we live in. We come now to another modern mystic of a quite different type.

Dag Hammarskjöld (1905-1961) is best known from the fact that for the last eight and a half years of his life he was the Secretary General of the United Nations. Before that time, he was a professional civil servant with extensive training in both law and economics, and held a number of important public offices in Sweden. His duties in all of these were performed with much proficiency, in which professional training, natural brilliance, a gift for diplomacy, and a prodigious capacity for work contributed to his success. Yet before his tragic death in a plane accident in September, 1961, as he was endeavoring to negotiate a settlement in the Congo, no one would have thought of him as a mystic.

What brought the inner Dag Hammarskjöld to light was the discovery of his private diary, which had been kept with many revelations of his inmost thoughts over a period of thirty-six years. Published with the title of *Markings*[22] and read by thousands, this gave the world a quite different Dag Hammarskjöld than had previously been visible. It consisted largely of apparently disconnected jottings, yet with an inner consistency that when read in sequence makes it possible to reconstruct from it the author's inner spiritual pilgrimage.

It had always been well known that Hammarskjöld was not a very sociable person in the "hail-fellow-well-met" sense, though agreeable and friendly enough when the occasion called for it. He had never married, and lived at home when his public duties permitted until he was forty.

What the *Markings* revealed was that he had long been a very lonely person. He felt alienated from God, from himself, and from other people. The book says nothing of his public career, but this seems to have been his only antidote to loneliness. We find him confessing "the anguish of loneliness . . . the same continual loneliness . . . the loneliness which is the final lot of all." [23] But again we find him writing of "work as an anesthetic against loneliness, books as a substitute for people—." [24]

This is not to imply that he had no thoughts of God, or of a duty to society, during this period. He was eager to live his life constructively, and he writes, "Pray that your loneliness may spur you into finding something to live for, great enough to die for." [25] He undertook the study of Albert Schweitzer's *Quest of the Historical Jesus,* and this led to meditations on Jesus and "the road that might lead to the Cross." Yet up to the years just preceding his election as Secretary General of the United Nations, he seems to have found no real release for his soul. In fact, the darker sentiments recorded in the years 1950 to 1952 seem to indicate that he was passing through what John of the Cross called "the dark night of the soul." [26]

Then something happened, though we do not know just when or how, and thereafter we find him able to say Yes to God and to his own soul. In a notation written in his diary on Whitsunday, 1961, we find these words:

> I don't know Who—or what—put the question, I don't know when it was put. I don't even remember answering. But at some moment I did answer *Yes* to Someone—or Something—and from that hour I was certain that existence is meaningful and that, therefore, my life, in self-surrender, had a goal.[27]

Though he attempts to give no day or hour, much less the year, of this change within him, it has been estimated from other references that it probably occurred toward the end of 1952. In any case, on New Year's, 1953, he was able to write in his diary some words that have been quoted so often as to have become almost a classic:

> For all that has been—Thanks!
> To all that shall be—Yes! [28]

It is a Yes mood that predominates in his writing from then on. Furthermore, he begins from that point to speak again and again of God—almost a hundred times of his being in the hands of God, or of "Not I, but God in me." [29]

Though reticent still about talking much publicly about his inner life, in a radio address prepared for the Edward R. Murrow program in 1953, he gave some significant references to major influences in his life. After paying tribute to his father's sense of duty and his mother's evangelical religious background as important childhood influences, he gives high credit to Albert Schweitzer's "ethical mysticism," with its selfless service and reverence for life. Furthermore, he mentions several of the medieval mystics in which self-surrender had become the way to self-realization. Elsewhere in *Markings,* he speaks particularly of Meister Eckhart, John of the Cross, and Thomas à Kempis; then of Blaise Pascal in the seventeenth century and of Martin Buber in the twentieth as having taught him how to combine the active with the contemplative life. So it may well be that these and some others dealt with in this book were on his bedside reading table!

Another evidence that the turning-point came in 1952 is the fact that after that time, the Bible, especially the Gospels and the Psalms, has a more frequent place in his diary. Whatever his other sources of inspiration, Jesus mattered most. A short time before its final entries he wrote, "As I continued along the Way, I learned, step by step, word by word, that behind every saying in the Gospels stands *one* man and *one* man's experience."[30]

Hammarskjöld, even after what must in traditional terms be called his conversion, was never a man to talk much about religion. Yet he was of no mind to deny to any the validity and richness of their faith. One evidence is "A Room for Quiet" which he insisted on having placed in the United Nations building so that all might have a place to worship according to whatever their faith might be. It was Hammarskjöld who said that "the more faithfully you listen to the voice within you, the better you will hear what is sounding outside. And only he who listens can speak."[31] That he did a great deal of effective speaking in his eight years as Secretary General is a matter of history. That he truly worshiped in those years, with a deep and mystical sense of God's presence, seems hardly open to question.

There is a citation in *Markings* that seems to say this so simply and clearly that I find no doubt about it, and hence do not hesitate to think of Dag Hammarskjöld as a twentieth-century mystic even though he did not announce this to the world. It is a prayer which I need daily to offer up to God in my much simpler life—and do we not all?

> Give me a pure heart—that I may see Thee,
> A humble heart—that I may hear Thee,
> A heart of love—that I may serve Thee,
> A heart of faith—that I may abide in Thee.[32]

The reader will understand that I have not in any sense attempted to give a complete compendium of the great mystics of the twentieth century. At least a dozen more who are widely known—perhaps more nearly twenty—might well have been included. I have chosen an apostle to the illiterates; a humanitarian greatly concerned for the poverty, hunger, and suffering of his country; a philosopher-scientist who saw the total universe as God's world and Christ the answer to its evil; and one of the most eminent and dedicated statesmen of our time as examples of what a deep and indwelling sense of God's presence can make of a man, and through him of his service to the world.

I have purposely selected as these examples four men who are no longer living. But the mysticism which undergirded their lives has been alive for many centuries, and it is not yet dead. What is it doing in our own day? What is real and what, perchance, is false about its modern forms? This must be our inquiry in the final chapter.

# VIII

# Neo-Mysticism Today

At the beginning of this book it was noted that mysticism fluctuates in its popularity. Furthermore, there are wide variations within classical mysticism, as the preceding surveys have indicated, yet with common elements. We come now to the most recent upturn in mystical interest, though it is doubtful that all of it is really mysticism. It may be viewed as pseudo-mystical, semi-mystical, or truly mystical but with departures from the long-standing mystical tradition.

To anticipate for the sake of identification, I regard as pseudo-mystical, and a bogus counterfeit, the popular vogue of astrology, clairvoyance, withcraft, magic, demonology, incantations, charms and amulets, and most of the visions and voices. The latter, we have noted, may sometimes accompany mystical experience but they do not constitute it. In the semi-mystical class are some quite radically different phenomena with a common center, the drug-induced "trip" with a mystical aura and the emergence of "the Jesus people" who have renounced drugs. Perhaps here also we should put the "celebrations" which have been substituted for traditional worship in many places, both in church services and elsewhere, for, says Harvey Cox, "Mysticism is not always serene and placid. It can become noisy, Dionysiac, even orgiastic." [1] More centrally in the long mystical tradition, when they are vital contemplative experiences and not merely faddist imitations of the Eastern religions, are Yoga and Zen. And speaking in tongues seems to be on the upsurge. In this chapter we shall take brief looks at all of these, though not entirely in this order.

## 1. How Has It Come About?

The taproot of these variations of life-style is to be found in the social conditions of our time. Overshadowing all else is the war with its violence, dislocations, aborting of the hopes of the young, breeding of a sense of injustice in the disparity of its burdens, and deep critical questions as to its morality. This touches all of us, but especially the young. Add to it the threat of atomic and ecological destruction which hangs over the planet and their futures, and there is further unrest. Add, again, the failure of a culture rooted in technology to contribute to the deeper values of life, whether in inner satisfactions or the increase of justice among men, and the young tend either to withdraw from their inherited patterns of life or to become militant in their attempt to change them. Mysticism of some sort is one response; confrontation is another.

These young people for the most part are from comfortable middle-class homes, with parents who are at least nominal church members. More than a few have been baptized and as children attended Sunday school or the equivalent Roman Catholic forms of instruction. Yet they have never found in their churches or their homes anything that gripped or molded them as a contagious religious influence. Or, having had it, they lost it under the pull of their peer group.

I said "nominal" church members. More often than not, this is the situation. But it is not always the case with the parents of these youth. It is unfair to genuinely committed Christians to suggest that there must be something wrong with them when their children follow the mores of the counter-culture. The causes are too complex for superficial judgment.

These young people who do not follow their inherited patterns of dress, deportment, or religion are often lonely. They believe, whether justly or not, that their parents do not understand them. The youth group in the church does not give them any deep fellowship, and the adults of the church, quite likely including the minister, seem to live in a different world. They do not lack for people around them, or for recreational things to do. There is plenty of excitement and electronic noise-making. They laugh and dance, play their record albums, and engage in sports. But on the inside nothing greatly satisfies or affords companionship and purpose for the soul.

These same young people, as Sabatier long ago put it in oft-quoted words, are "incurably religious." They may turn their backs on the church, or have their doubts about God, or claim to be atheists. But still, they believe there must be Something—

a Force if not a Being, that controls the world and can give satisfaction to their lives. To the degree that this conviction grips them, they set themselves to finding what it is. When the channels are open which seem to lead in this direction, they enter them. It is then that they are drawn toward mysticism of one kind or another.

There are, of course, persons in this group who are "after thirty." Yet, on the whole, the neo-mysticism of today is a phenomenon of the young, and unlike the past, of persons who have not had long or deep previous experience of a religious nature.

## 2. The Pseudo-Mysticism of the Occult

As was stated at the outset, mysticism needs to be clearly distinguished from superstition, astrology, incantation, and every kind of pseudo-science as well as pseudo-religion. It roots in the mystery of the meeting between God and the human spirit, but not in attempts to manipulate the Ultimate, whether to claim what one desires to have or to know, or to exorcise some evil thing.

This would not be worth mentioning further, save for common misunderstandings. These are reflected all around us, as is the mysterious lure of the occult. In a scientific age, why do hundreds of daily newspapers print a syndicated horoscope? Does anyone really believe that the location of the stars on the day of one's birth determines his destiny? Apparently some do. With all that is now known of psychology and sociology, why believe in demonology and witchcraft? Why do otherwise intelligent modern Americans appear to believe in voodoo charms, locks of hair, candles, beads, flowers, lotions and potions, to ward off danger and ensure good luck?

The most charitable answer is that to some people such acts and objects are symbols of the unseen powers which in some way are related to the presence of God. One thing, however, all this makes clear. This is that even in a scientific and technological age, science is not everything. Mysticism says that also, but because mysticism and astrology agree at this point does not make astrology mysticism.

There are various answers to the questions posed above.

Some persons doubtless yield to superstition because they have never outgrown it. Others may espouse a false mysticism because its truer forms call for a painful self-discipline. Probably many take to the occult through a desperate hope that these things *might* work when nothing else seems to afford inner satisfaction. The frequency of such procedures is a symbol of both the desperation of large segments of society and of the failure of religious agencies to impart a firm and reasonable faith for tough times.

## 3. The Drug Route to Mystical Experience

The attempt to escape by way of drugs from the humdrum
ld of every day to a realm of fantastic beauty and delight
very long history. "Psychedelic drugs have been known
people of India for centuries. . . . Of course, it is no secret
e drugs do produce psychic visions and experiences—
in powers." [2] So, too in the American Southwest the
tops of the mescal cactus, or peyote, were chewed by
in their religious ceremonies, and the mescaline of
ntinuity from this practice.
as 1874, Benjamin Blood began to promote what
anaesthetic revolution," claiming that he had
into "the genius of being" by experiments in
oused the interest of William James, and
try some experiments himself. One of these
led to "the tremendously exciting sense of an
al illumination," which disappeared as the
cal wore off; another with a peyote button
ly sick. In the *Varieties of Religious Experi-*
possibility of inducing by drugs something
cal experience, but without giving it full

nducement to "consciousness-changing"
h closer to our own time. In 1943 in a
in Basel a Swiss chemist, Albert Hof-
king on a compound of lysergic acid
lly swallowed a small amount of it.
"trip." This is how he described it.

> On arriving home I lay down in a dazed condition with my eyes closed. There surged upon me an uninterrupted stream of fantasic images of extraordinary plasticity and vividness and accompanied by an intense, kaleidoscopic play of colors. I felt a marked desire to laugh. I had great difficulty in speaking coherently, my field of vision swayed before me, and objects appeared distorted like images in curved mirrors. The faces of those around me appeared as grotesque, colored masks. I had a clear recognition of my condition, in which state I sometimes observed, in the manner of an independent, neutral observer, that I shouted half insanely or babbled incoherent words. Occasionally I felt as if I were out of my body. All acoustic perceptions (e.g., the noise of a passing car) were transformed into optical effects, every sound evoking a corresponding colored hallucination constantly changing in shape and color.[4]

At first no direct connection was made between this fantastic experience and mysticism. This came in 1954 when Aldous Huxley, well-known author and exponent of mysticism in *The Perennial Philosophy*, published *The Doors of Perception*. In this book he told how his experiments with mescaline had made the "I" become "Not-Self," and had caused ordinary objects to glow with jewel-like colors that seemed to have an inner mean-ing in a world of transcendental experience. Thereafter he con tinued to use mescaline and LSD occasionally in conjunctio with other forms of meditation, and came to regard their u as sacramental.

The next stage developed in the early 1960s when Timot Leary, who taught clinical psychology at Harvard, began promote the use of LSD, not only as a consciousness-chang drug in times of boredom or other malaise but as having relig significance. His formula, "Turn on. Tune in. Drop out," came a familiar byword. Psychedelic experiments were se in which, among others, Aldous Huxley, Gerald Heard, Alan Watts participated. Watts gave the next major pu the direction of psychedelic mysticism tinctured with Z his *Joyous Cosmology,* which appeared in 1962.

Throughout the 1960 decade the consumption of dr creased, sometimes with and more often without a r significance, until the drug problem reached the alarmi portions of today. That it is a desperately serious soc can hardly be questioned. But what shall we say of dru mystical consciousness?

When used by mature persons like those whose na

been mentioned, who already have a religious background and interest, I do not dispute the fact that it may have the effects they claim for this experience. As consciousness of the perils and distresses, or even of the humdrum familiar features, of the sense-bound world drops out, it is quite possible that a "joyous cosmology" akin to mystical ecstasy ensues. I have never tried it, but I accept the witness of those who have.

However, unless the drugs are used with a restraint such as immature young people are not likely to exercise, it is extremely dangerous to bodily, mental, and religious health. To borrow an analogy from an article in *Life* on "The Chemistry of Madness," [5] the brain with its billions of neurons is intended to work together like a symphony, not all its instruments in operation at one time but all harmonized to work together for intelligent thought. Two substances recently discovered, noradrenalin and dopamine, turn on the arousal structures of the brain and wake us up normally to greater alertness and activity. When LSD is taken into the system, these elements are greatly overstimulated, and the brain becomes uncontrollably aroused to experience hallucinations, sometimes pleasant and again terrifying. In short, the symphonic balance is no longer present; the person taking the drug is quite literally unbalanced, in what may seem either a mystical ecstasy or a "bad trip."

The resulting psychological and social dangers are well known. But what of the religious angle? Does it justify the risk? Is the euphoria, if it ensues, a true form of mystical experience? My answer is No. I shall attempt to say why.

In the first place, such a drug-induced "trip," even with a religious aura, endangers the body and mind, which ought to be dedicated to the service of God with all one's powers. There is a vital place for suffering in the Christian outlook, even upon occasion for "giving one's body to be burned," but not for burning one's body with chemicals in the hope of inducing an ecstatic sensation.

In the second place, it is selfish. Granted that the mystics of the classical tradition often sought inner peace rather than large-scale changes in society, they virtually always sought to relieve the suffering of others in their immediate situation. The quest for the beatific vision at the cost of much "self-naughting" has had a very different motivation from the drug-induced type.

True mysticism centers in God, not in a pleasurable feeling-tone.

A further difference lies in the after-effects. Drugs leave a hangover not unlike that resulting from alcohol, which is itself a drug with a similar disturbing effect on the brain. The practice of the presence of God leaves one better prepared for the service of God with a new sense of divinely given strength and energy.

The experience itself differs at a crucial point. The classical mystical rapture, though transient, shines with a steady glow of illumination while it lasts. The rapid fluctuation of hallucinatory sensations, even when said to be beautiful and "jewel-like," is something quite different.

Finally and in summation, its pragmatic effects discredit it. Swami Prabhavananda of the Vedanta center in Hollywood protests the use of hallucinogens both as his own opinion and that of Patanjali, three centuries before Christ:

> In fact, Patanjali, the father of Indian Yoga, has explicitly stated that "psychic powers may be obtained by drugs." But he also strongly warned that the use of such means can obstruct spiritual progress and block genuine spiritual experience. . . . The user of LSD may actually see a light enveloping the universe or sense the presence of God or a divine being. But as soon as the effects of the drug wear off, he finds himself spiritually dry and empty. . . . The simple but powerful language of the Bible expresses it succinctly: "By their fruits you shall know them." This is the basis for the evaluation of a spiritual experience.[6]

## 4. Vedanta and Yoga

Hindu religious thought goes commonly by the name of Vedanta, though this applies particularly to the Brahman religious philosophy and its accompaniments. This is much too complex to be covered adequately in a brief space, but I shall try to give its main outlines and indicate the route by which it came to this country.

Vedanta gets its name from the Vedas composed in the second millennium B.C. although they are not the only or the most influential part of the Hindu scriptures. They are sacrificial hymns of great richness and variety which reflect a pantheon of nature deities, of which Agni (Fire), Varuna (Rain), and Mitra (Sun) came to be regarded as the most important. They are still used in ritualistic worship, and the initials of these deities may be the source of the "Om" of repetitive Indian meditation.[7]

However, it was from the Upanishads which originated between 1000 (some say 800) and 500 B.C. that the Brahmanic faith was born. In these, polytheism gives way to a monistic idealism which is almost, if not quite, pantheistic. Brahman is the One, the Real, the Ground of all existence, eternal and unchanging Being, while the phenomenal world of change and appearance is nonbeing, which came to be called *maya*, or illusion. But what of the human self? Man's body and what he ordinarily means by "I" is equally unsubstantial but within him is Atman, the divine Self, which is also the Universal Self identical with Brahman. Thus it is possible for each person to say of himself, "That art Thou," and of another that he too is Brahman. Hence, "Yonder person I am He." [8]

With this nondualism, or *advaita,* as it was called by the Indian philosopher Sankara (A.D. 788-820), were linked reincarnation and karma. Each self had had a body many times before, and would again. While it could exercise its will in moral choices during each such incarnation, by the inexorable law of karma its status in the next life would be determined by its conduct in the present one. And how escape this otherwise endless chain of rebirths? By such meditation and other spiritual disciplines that the Atman within the self would blend with the Universal Self in an experience of union which brought indescribable peace, serenity, and joy. This ascent from consciousness to the superconscious is called *samadhi*.

This called for a method to be developed for bringing the empirical self into this transcendental state. This method was, and is, yoga. While present-day yoga has taken on elements not found in the original form, control of the breath with intense concentration on a single point seems to have had a very ancient history. A passage in the Bhagavad Gita represents Krishna as thus giving directions to his worshiper:

> A devotee should constantly devote himself to abstraction, remaining in a secret place, alone, with his mind and self restrained, without expectations and without belongings. . . . Holding his body, head, and neck even and unmoved, remaining steady, looking at the tip of his own nose, and not looking about in various directions, with a tranquil self, devoid of fear, he should restrain his mind and concentrate it on Me and sit down engaged in devotion, regarding Me as his final goal. Thus constantly devoting himself to abstraction, a devotee whose mind is restrained attains that tranquillity which culminates in final emancipation and assimilation with Me.[9]

The Bhagavad Gita, which dates from somewhere between 100 B.C. and A.D. 200, is a masterpiece of religious literature. It gives instructions not only for religious meditation but for personal devotion, or *bhakti,* and thus for love and action as part of the total religious life. It assumes the presence of *avatars,* or incarnations of deity, appearing in the human scene. Of these Krishna, the incarnation of Vishnu and the charioteer of Arjuna, is the central figure, and he is represented as addressing Arjuna to proclaim the truths of religion and suggest his duty. This not only expands the philosophy of the Upanishads but paves the way for an eclecticism by which both the Buddha and the Christ could also be regarded as avatars.

We must now look at how this Indian faith and practice came to America. It stems from the influence of Sri Ramakrishna, (1836-1886) a Hindu saint and scholar thoroughly conversant with the other major religions, whose holy living led to his being regarded as an avatar. One of his disciples, Swami Vivekananda, brought Vedanta to America and founded the Ramakrishna Order. Coming first as a delegate to the Parliament of Religions at the World's Columbian Exposition in Chicago in 1893, he traveled and lectured widely with the result that Vedanta Centers were founded in a considerable number of cities.

Three of the most important of these centers were founded in Los Angeles, Boston, and New York, later to be presided over respectively by Swamis Prabhavananda, Akhilananda, and Nikhilananda (*ananda* means "the blessed one"). These men have exerted wide influence by writing and speaking on Hindu psychology and religion and how they are related to Western Christianity. It is no longer the novelty it once was to see swamis in saffron-colored robes lecturing on how to achieve *samadhi* and on points of contact between Eastern and Western faith if Christ be regarded as an avatar.

Three other men, not swamis but literary figures with England as their native land, have been ardent students of Vedanta and have done much to spread the knowledge of it in America. These are Aldous Huxley, Gerald Heard, and Christopher Isherwood. Huxley and Heard, we noted, experimented with drug-induced mysticism but their interest in Indian religious philosophy went much deeper. This appears in many of their books, though it is not always thus designated. I recall participating along with Heard at a Quaker retreat in the 1940s, listening to his brilliant addresses, and wondering how much of this was Christian. I did not then recognize that it was Vedanta superimposed upon a blend of emergent evolution[10] and Anglican mysticism, though it clearly was something quite different from my middle-of-the-road Christian liberalism (to which the Quakers listened politely but with much less fascination).

The best known exponent of Indian mystical thought and practice today is Maharishi Mahesh Yogi, who has traveled in this country. At his ashram in India he became the guru, or teacher, of such famous figures in the entertainment world as the Beatles and Mia Farrow, though I believe none of them completed his course of instruction. He teaches a simple inner quest for peace of mind that he calls "transcendental meditation." For a donation of thirty-five dollars per person, thousands of American college students have attempted to become transcendental meditators. His requirement of abstention from drugs has been one good effect of the movement.

Yoga has come along with the rest of Vedanta, though often as a popular practice not much connected with its philosophical and religious origins. It is of various types. The swamis mentioned above discuss four forms of it as spiritual disciplines: bhakti yoga, seeking God in personal devotion through love; karma yoga, the selfless performance of work and action; jnana-yoga, knowledge of God through philosophical reflection; and raja yoga, realization of the Self through mind-control and concentrated meditation, somewhat as specified by Patanjali many centuries ago. These have differing focuses but are not mutually exclusive.[11]

Hatha yoga, from *ha* (sun) and *tha* (moon), is a less sophisticated type which aims to bring the positive and negative energies of the self into a balanced harmony. It lays much emphasis on bodily postures (*asanas*), on proper breathing (*pranayama*), on right thoughts, right actions and proper concentration, and on affirmations of faith and truth called *mantras*. With the emphasis given to breathing and physical agility, such as standing on one's head and using normally unused muscles, it is sometimes identified with gymnastics. Its purpose, however, is not physical fitness only but an integration of the physical, mental, and spiritual components of personhood.

Another legacy from Indian religion is the Hare Krishna, or Krishna Consciousness, movement. This differs from Vedanta in that it finds its main source not in the Upanishads, but in the Bhagavad Gita and the worship of Krishna as the incarnation of God. Thus, the Gita is substituted for the Bible and Krishna for Christ. This makes of it a direct protest against the Establishment, the churches, and the Christian faith in which many of its exponents were reared. At the downtown business center of one of the larger cities one may hear a group of young Americans in saffron robes chanting:

Hare Krishna, Hare Krishna,
Krishna, Krishna, Hare, Hare!
Hare Rama, Hare Rama,
Rama, Rama, Hare, Hare!

These praises are anything but the silent prayers usually associated with mystical meditation, and it is doubtful that this should be called mysticism. Yet it is said to clear the dust from one's soul, banish the *maya* which separates one from God, and bring the chanter into closer relation with God by invoking Krishna and thus evoking the Krishna Consciousness. Perhaps. What is certain is that these young people, unlike the Jesus people whom we shall discuss later, find their object of devotion outside of the Christian tradition instead of within it.

## 5. Zen Buddhism

A different type of Eastern religion, imported not from India but Japan, is Zen. It is a sect of Mahayana Buddhism. It was developed in China in the sixth century, where it took on some elements of Taoism, and in Japan in the twelfth, but it did not reach America to any great extent until the twentieth. At the World Parliament of Religions in Chicago in 1893 it was expounded by the Buddhist Abbot Soyen Shaku. But its most influential expositor was to be his disciple, D. T. Suzuki (1870-1966), who during his long life wrote many books on the subject, of which the best known is his *Mysticism: Christian and Buddhist* in which he finds similarities between Zen and the thought of Meister Eckhart.[12] He lived in the United States from 1897 to 1909 and again from 1947 to 1957, teaching at

Columbia as professor of religion in the latter period. Another person who has done much to interpret and popularize Zen is Alan Watts, whom I first knew as the Episcopal student chaplain at Northwestern University in the 1940s. He had already written *The Spirit of Zen* (1936), introducing Zen to the English-reading public. This was followed by a number of other books in this field, of which *The Way of Zen* (1959) [13] departs somewhat from his earlier writing to try to make Zen more consistent with the prevailing scientific mood.

To understand Zen even in outline, it is necessary to review its ancient backgrounds. As is well known, Buddhism is an offshoot of the religion of India, though no longer the faith of the land of its birth. It owes its origin to Prince Siddhartha, better known as Gautama the Buddha, "the enlightened one," who lived approximately between 560 and 480 B.C. Deeply troubled over the sorrows of the world, he left his family and sought unsuccessfully for five years through yoga and extreme asceticism to solve the problem of evil. One day as he sat beneath the pipal (bodhi) tree he found enlightenment. This spiritual insight gave him peace, serenity, and a life of compassion and humble service for the remainder of his long life. This insight was embodied in the "four noble truths," of which the essential note of the first three is the finding of happiness through the conquest of desire, and the fourth is the "noble eight-fold path" of right views, resolve, speech, conduct, livelihood, effort, mindfulness, and contemplation.

The last two of these "paths" links the way of the Buddha with mysticism. It is through mindful concentration that insight is gained for right living. Buddhism is more than mystical contemplation; it relates to the totality of life. As the Buddha set forth his message, it is the Middle Way between asceticism and worldly living, and it leads to compassion, to peace of mind, to enlightenment, and to nirvana.

Buddhism differs at important points from its Hindu background, which accounts for its moving out to take root elsewhere. It has no God such as the Universal Self of Brahman or the Atman within the individual soul. In fact, it has no soul as an individual entity, only an onflowing stream of consciousness, such as David Hume and after him other Western philosophers centuries later were to assert. There were no avatars or other gods to be worshiped. The Buddha himself never claimed to be one, though his followers were later to deify him. Transmigration and karma were retained from the Hindu background. The *dharma* of Brahmanic religion had enjoined resignation to suffering, and this included acceptance of one's caste as his predestined lot in life. Buddhism transformed this into a new *dhamma* which broke with the caste system and offered hope to any who would follow the way of the four noble truths. This was a major factor in its becoming a missionary religion.

What Buddhism substituted for the other elements it rejected was a very strong emphasis on nirvana—a state of blessedness which could not only put an end to the wheel of rebirths but could be won in the present life. The result was essentially an ethical system but practiced with great intensity and devotion.

Buddhism split into two main groups—the Theravada, which its detractors called Hinayana (the Lesser Vehicle), and the Mahayana (the Greater Vehicle). The former was the more conservative branch, and spread through Southeast Asia. It emphasized the importance of personal saintliness, and hence of the monastic brotherhood. Mahayana Buddhism became entrenched in China, Japan, and Korea, and stressed not only nirvana but a devout life of self-sacrifice and compassion. It developed the idea of *Bodhisattvas,* who were content to defer the future state of nirvana to help their fellowmen by repeated incarnations. In popular thought many of these, like the Buddha himself, became deified.

Zen as an outgrowth of Mahayana Buddhism retains this ideal of compassion and love of the brother. But it is also a religion of self-power, or self-realization, which puts great emphasis on meditation as a channel to personal peace and serenity. We must now look at it in its current modes.

The basic note of Zen is *satori,* a mystical experience of enlightment. Suzuki says of this that it is "the Alpha and Omega of Zen Buddhism. Zen devoid of satori is like a sun without its light and heat." [14] It is conceived as entrance into Buddhahood, the enlightenment which is both the discovery of truth and the transformation of life. *Satori* is to be sought, so its advocates maintain, to find clarity of purpose and enhancement of selfhood within the confusions and strains of living in the space-time world.

The three pillars of Zen, so-called, are teaching, practice, and enlightenment,[15] all under the instruction of a Zen master. Right living is emphasized, for has not the Buddha said, "The man who walks in the noble path lives in the world, and yet his heart is not defiled by worldly desires"? [16] Contemplation aims to develop a basic attitude toward all things.

Yet the most distinctive elements of Zen are the *zazen* and the *koan*. In the *zazen* one sits in meditation, preferably in the lotus position with the legs crossed, the spine erect, the breathing regulated, and the mind shutting out all distracting thoughts. To do this one may concentrate on his breathing in order to suppress thoughts of family, work, play, or other distractions, and if successful the *satori* may result.

The *koan* is a difficult problem posed by the Zen master, often in the form of an enigma with a paradoxical twist, which must be solved by the pupil if he is to have *satori*. An illustration sometimes cited is that the pupil must explain how it is that the wild geese have flown away, while the master declares that they are still here, and always have been. The *satori* comes when the disciple recognizes that the answer lies not in logic but in an intuitive certainty that he lives in a Reality that transcends the world of time and space.

What is this Reality? It is clearly not a personal God, nor is it the Absolute of Hegelian idealism. Suzuki says its comes closest to being the Emptiness, or Godhead, of Meister Eckhart. But in Zen this is without the breakthrough of the Christian Trinity. It is the luminous Darkness from which comes enlightenment for the redirection and stabilization of life.

Suzuki has spelled out eight characteristics of the mystical *satori* which form an interesting comparison with the four of William James. These he designates as irrationality, intuitive insight, authoritativeness, affirmation, a sense of the Beyond, its impersonal tone, a feeling of exaltation, and momentariness.[17] By irrationality he means that *satori* is not a conclusion to be reached by reasoning and it defies intellectual analysis. Intuitive insight is the noetic quality stressed by William James. Its authoritativeness is its finality, irrefutable by logic, to the person who experiences it. It is essentially an affirmative attitude of acceptance toward all things when they are seen in their transcendental aspect. (Suzuki denies that this is pantheism.) The sense of the Beyond means that the experience is individual, but in *satori* the encasement of personality melts away into something greater than itself, with a sense of complete release or rest. It has no personal note such as is found in Christian mysticism. It does, however, have a comparable feeling of exaltation through breaking away from the restrictions of individual being. It comes abruptly and suddenly, though there may have been long preparation for it, and it may come even in the midst of one's daily occupation.[18]

What shall we make of all this? Not having been personally instructed in Zen, I think I should have difficulty with the *zazen* and *koan* elements of it. Nor am I sufficiently divorced from the demands of rational coherence, or from faith in the God who through Christ is more than Emptiness, to find deep satisfactions in pursuing this channel. Yet I do not question that Zen has religious as well as ethical values that give it a strong appeal to many, not only of the East, but of those whose cultural background is Western. The unspeakableness of God is not new or wholly alien to Christian theology. And in a dark and crippling world where any ray of light, or source of a stronger selfhood, is eagerly seized upon, it is not strange that Zen has brought rest and peace to many.

In spite of acknowledged values in fruitful forms of discipline, Zen does not provide a substitute for Christianity nor is it possible to speak without contradiction of "Christian Zen." In its mysticism there are important points of contact; yet in theological structure there are basic differences which color the rest of the systems. The God of Christian faith is a personal God of love, goodness, wisdom, and creativity, known in spite of our human ignorance through Jesus Christ. In the Christian view of nature as the ongoing creation of God it is not something to blend into, as in Zen, but to use for human good with an active obligation to make it the substructure of a better world. The Judeo-Christian view of history has a *past* giving stable direction from a long heritage and a *future* affording hope through the power and the promise of God as well as an inward present of meditative insight. Thus the meeting-points in mystical experience take on radically different colorations.

## 6. The Celebration

In sharp contrast with these meditative modern revivals of ancient mystical practices from the East is the present vogue, both within the churches and in rock festivals, of celebration. Because it is now a familiar occurrence and because it stands on the borderline of mystical experience, I shall deal with it more briefly than the preceding.

Celebration is not a new word in religious diction, for the priests of communions with a formal liturgy have long since "celebrated" the sacrament of the Lord's Supper, while Methodists and some others of the free church persuasion have simply "administered" the sacraments. We are told that long centuries ago David danced before the Lord (II Sam. 6:14), and in one of the loveliest of the psalms we are enjoined:

> Praise him with trumpet sound;
> praise him with lute and harp!
> Praise him with timbrel and dance;
> praise him with strings and pipe!
> Praise him with sounding cymbals;
> praise him with loud clashing cymbals!
> Let everything that breathes praise the Lord!
> Praise the Lord!
>
> (Psalm 150:3-6)

In consonance with this spirit and in expression of the joy in the Lord felt by the worshipers, these injunctions have often been followed, with such modifications as the culture prompted. There is nothing new about loud music, the clapping of hands, or the dance in religious worship, though some of its more bizarre forms are new. Usually this exuberance has been regarded as a form of praise, but hardly of mystical quest. Today we are experiencing a new development in the fact that in such celebrations, praise and prayer, excitement and solemnity, the adoration of the Lord and the embrace of one another, are so mingled that the distinction between them breaks down.

Harvey Cox in *The Feast of Fools* makes much of the fact that festival and fantasy are integral parts of religion, as they should be in wholesome human living. He finds in the rock music, bright costumes, and exuberant dancing of the young today a form of neo-mysticism. Says he, "Festivity and contemplation are close cousins. The things that make life contemplative are the same things that make life celebrative: the capacity to step back from tasks and chores, the ability to 'hang-loose' from merely material goods, the readiness to relish an experience on its own terms." [19] Cox also makes the interesting suggestion that the withdrawal from sense impressions by silence and solitude in the older mysticism is now being accomplished though such overstimulation by electronic music, flashing lights, and the "mind-blowing" effects of the multi-media that the senses fail to take in that with which they are bombarded.[20]

Shall we agree with this analysis? Some kinds of festivity can certainly be blended with a holy joy and praise to the Lord for his goodness. Christian worship may be either silent or stupendously soundful, but it ought never to be drab or dismal. The three basic requirements of public worship are reverence, dignity, and fitness, and it need not be traditional in order to be vital and genuine. I have participated in some novel forms of celebration in worship that meet these requirements, and have witnessed others that do not.

Yet some distinctions need to be kept clear. Festivity for entertainment is not the same thing as festive worship. Furthermore, a celebration may be legitimately festive without being mystical, for mysticism is not the whole of religion. Festivity and contemplation may have some common elements without being identical or even "close cousins."

Again we had better apply the test, "By their fruits you shall know them." Does the celebration aim to bring the worshiper into a direct and immediate sense of the presence of God? Above the sound and light does he perceive a divine companionship and feel an inner guidance to better living? Does the experience broaden his horizons, deepen his insights, and prompt him to a greater love of God, a greater moral obedience, a greater sensitivity to the needs of others? Does it stress suffering and the cost of discipleship as well as joy? If so, I should be willing to call it a mystical experience. If not, it is too apt to be a sensory stimulating form of entertainment engaged in primarily for hedonistic rather than spiritual motives.

## 7. The Jesus Movement

We come now to what is perhaps the most amazing of all the amazing movements of our time—the emergence into prominence of "the Jesus people," or as they sometimes call themselves, "the Jesus freaks." There are thousands of them today, virtually all of them college age or younger, witnessing and evangelizing on the streets, on campuses, and sometimes in churches.

What has emerged is apparently a youth movement with the zeal and some of the methods of Hare Krishna but with Jesus, not Krishna, in the center of it; a form of celebration that is innovative but with much traditional substance; and a counterculture that like the Eastern religions speaks out against drugs and for a more satisfying personal religion than its adherents see in the religion of their parents.

Those in the Jesus movement are not all of one pattern, save in their zeal for Jesus and a newly found Christian conversion. They are from all churches and from none, and from all kinds of educational, economic, and social backgrounds. An extended article in *Time*[21] classifies them as the Jesus People, which includes mainly the Street Christians as an offshoot of the hippie movement; the Straight People in the evangelical campus and other youth groups such as the Campus Crusade for Christ, the Inter-Varsity Christian Fellowship and Youth for Christ; and the Catholic Pentecostals, publicly loyal to their church but meeting privately in homes for ecstatic and charismatic worship. The first of these groups has attracted most attention, for the second has long been active, and the third, while disturbing to some of the hierarchy of their church, has received less publicity.

With such differences, any description will fit some forms of the movement but not others. Yet there is a common pattern. These convictions seem paramount: that Jesus saves, and has saved these young people to a new meaning and purpose in life; that Jesus calls them to witness to their faith on every possible occasion and in every available manner; that the Bible is their one source of truth and authority.

The result is commonly observable phenomena: much singing of gospel songs both old and new, with the playing of records in this vein and an occasional rock festival; street witnessing by preaching, conversation, and printed matter; parades with banners extolling the love of Jesus; the Jesus symbol—a raised fist with the forefinger pointing upward; the issuance of their own

## 8. Speaking in Tongues

It would hardly be appropriate to end the chapter—or the book—without saying something of a very ancient practice that is now experiencing a revival of interest. To speak in unintelligible syllables as a form of Christian witness is technically called glossolalia, though more commonly spoken of as "the gift of tongues." It used to be almost exclusively the prerogative of the Pentecostal sects. Of late, however, "the charismatic revival," of which this is one expression, has made its way into the mainline churches and speaking in tongues is practiced by some in almost every denomination, and sometimes in seminaries, colleges, or other intellectual centers. What are we to make of it?

It is still so controversial a subject that I have no expectation of full agreement with what I shall say about it. What I shall attempt will be to say what it is, with something of its biblical background, and after a few words as to the reasons for its growing popularity, try to relate it to the mysticism we have been considering throughout the book.

In the first place, the word "charismatic" is an ambiguous term, much broader in its meaning than speaking in tongues. "Charismata" literally means "things freely given." In the New Testament it means the gifts or new forms of life bestowed by the Spirit on the Christian. The capacity for speaking in tongues is mentioned as one of them, but not the only one, and not the most important of them. This becomes clearly evident in I Corinthians 12:4-11. "Now there are varieties of gifts, but the same Spirit; and there are varieties of service, but the same Lord; and there are varieties of working, but it is the same God who inspires them all in every one" (vss.4-6). Then Paul enumerates ten such gifts, which include the utterance of wisdom, knowledge, faith, gifts of healing, and others until he concludes with "various kinds of tongues" and "the interpretation of tongues."

It is in I Corinthians 14 that Paul deals with the subject most fully. Without condemning the practice, he makes such observations as, "He who speaks in a tongue edifies himself, but he who prophesies edifies the church" (vs. 4). "And if the bugle gives an indistinct sound, who will get ready for battle? So with yourselves; if you in a tongue utter speech that is not intelligible, how will anyone know what is said? For you will be speaking into the air" (vss. 8, 9). Then he clinches the matter with the words, "I thank God that I speak in tongues more than you all; nevertheless, in church I would rather speak five words with my mind, in order to instruct others, than ten thousand words in a tongue" (vss. 18, 19).

To such words as these from Paul must be added the fact that, in spite of the account in Acts 2, the practice of speaking in tongues has a minor place in the New Testament as a whole. It was Peter's great sermon on Pentecost (Acts 2:14-36), or Stephen's moving address just before his martyrdom (Acts 7:2-53), or the innumerable addresses of Paul and the other apostles, that had most to do with the birth of the church and the bringing of the gift of new life in Christ to their hearers.

What I gather from this biblical evidence is that while the speaking in tongues in our time, or any other, is not forbidden, neither is it advocated. Whatever its legitimacy, it ought not to be supposed that it brings a "baptism of the Spirit" that is not as well or better obtained through other channels. And the best of all is what Paul in I Corinthians 12:31 calls "a still more excellent way."

Why has glossolalia emerged in our time? Perhaps, like most of what has been surveyed in this chapter, it is a fad which will have its day and pass. But there may be a deeper reason. The distinguished pastoral psychologist Wayne Oates suggests that it may be because we have so largely made a taboo of serious discussion of religion in our homes, schools, social contacts, and even churches that the repressed emotional feeling, latent in the subconscious but finding no normal outlet, bursts forth in this form.[24] It seems reasonable to suppose that when one finds himself in a group where others are speaking in tongues, the taboo is lifted and he speaks with greater feeling than he could in the more generally accepted religious verbiage. In any case, if we talked about our deep thoughts regarding religion more often in our ordinary situations, there might be less sense of need for the expression of feeling in a special manner.

But is glossolalia a form of mysticism? Is it a kind of mystical ecstasy? An authentic sign of the Spirit's presence? It depends on the individual's temperament and on other aspects of his religious experience. It depends especially on his accepting and using fruitfully all the other "gifts of the Spirit" of which Paul spoke, and most of all, his acceptance of "the more excellent way" of love in all his relationships. To wish to speak in tongues mainly to demonstrate to others that one has received "the baptism of the Spirit" can be a form of self-righteous pride. To speak in tongues because one feels that in this way he can say best what is deepest in his life, and then demonstrates in his total living that he lives in the presence of God and by the light of the Spirit, is quite another matter, and one that I have no wish to disparage.

This book has been written by a lifelong Methodist of Quaker ancestry. This may account for the fact that I have had occasion to do a considerable amount of speaking, whether by scheduled appointment or "as the Spirit moves." I have never spoken in tongues, and doubt that I am likely to. If the reader wishes to examine it from the inside by one who has, I recommend the reading of Marcus Bach's fascinating story of his experience, *The Inner Ecstasy.* [25]

And now this book must end, leaving untouched large areas of mystical history and literature. I trust that enough has been said to demonstrate that authentic Christian mysticism has a very vital meaning and message for our time.

We live in a new age and must expect to have new experiences, but we disregard at our peril the spiritual wisdom of the past. It both gives us guidelines and points toward new guidelines for our day. Most of all, it sets before us a Guide. As truly as in the early days of the church, Jesus Christ is Lord. His promise of the coming of the Spirit has been fulfilled throughout the centuries. Like those of old, we too can say with a life-giving assurance, "Come, Holy Spirit."

# Notes

## I. Definitions and Distinctions

1. A. E. Wiggam, *The New Decalogue of Science* (Indianapolis: Bobbs-Merrill, 1923), p. 262.
2. Rufus M. Jones, *The Testimony of the Soul* (New York: Macmillan, 1936), p. 200.
3. Dom Cuthbert Butler, *Western Mysticism* (London: Constable, 1922), pp. 3-4.
4. W. R. Inge, *Mysticism in Religion* (London: Hutchinson's Universal Library), p. 8.
5. Rufus M. Jones, *Studies in Mystical Religion* (London: Macmillan, 1909), p. xv. Italics his.
6. These are recounted by Hal Bridges in *American Mysticism from William James to Zen* (New York: Harper, 1970), pp. 26-28. Rufus Jones's close relation with his son Lowell, including the circumstances connected with his death, is told in *The Luminous Trail* (New York: Macmillan, 1947), Chap. XIV.
7. Jones, *The Luminous Trail,* p. 26, *The Radiant Life* (New York: Macmillan, 1944), p. 94.
8. Evelyn Underhill, *Mysticism* (London: Methuen, 1911, 1930), p. 72.
9. *Western Mysticism,* p. 5.
10. These excerpts are taken from Eckhart's *Sermons,* and are successively from Sermons 71, 79, 69, 10, 83.
11. Aldous Huxley, *The Perennial Philosophy* (New York: Harper, 1945.) Chapter I, entitled "That Art Thou" cites many illustrations from both Eastern and Western mysticism.
12. Quoted by Rufus Jones in *The Radiant Life,* p. 107.
13. For important expressions of this position see John B. Cobb, Jr., *God and the World* (Philadelphia: Westminster Press, 1969) and John A. T. Robinson *Exploration into God* (Stanford: Stanford University Press, 1967).
14. As in Rom. 16:25; I Cor. 2:7; Eph. 1:9; 3:3, 4, 9; 6:19; Col. 1: 26, 27; 4:3; I Tim. 3:9, 16.
15. *Confessions,* IX, 24. Its fuller context will be given later in Chapter IV, pp. 85-86.
16. This conjunction of pronouns occurs frequently in the anonymous *Theologia Germanica* of the fourteenth century which greatly influenced Martin Luther, though he relinquished the *via negativa* after his break with Catholicism.
17. Butler, *Western Mysticism,* p. ix.
18. William James, *The Varieties of Religious Experience: A Study in Human Nature* (London: Longmans, Green, 1902, 1928), pp. 380-82.
19. A. N. Whitehead, *Process and Reality* (New York: Macmillan, 1929), p. 532.
20. Thomas S. Kepler, *The Fellowship of the Saints* (New York and Nashville: Abingdon-Cokesbury Press, 1948).

21. Evelyn Underhill, *Mystimism,* p. 367.
22. Eugene W. Lyman, *The Meaning and Truth of Religion* (New York: Scribner's, 1933), pp. 110-12.
23. I mean by personalistic philosophy any intellectual system which has as its central focus a personal God and the dignity and worth of the human person. Its distinction from pantheism, in which some forms of mysticism are rooted, will be considered in Chapter III.

## II. Mysticism in the Bible

1. Abraham Joshua Heschel, *God in Search of Man: A Philosophy of Judaism* (New York: Farrar, Straus & Cudahy, 1955), pp. 225-26.
2. The term "spiritual marriage" appears with considerable frequency in medieval mystical writing, connoting a settled state of spiritual union with God. It did not suggest to these writers the morbid sexuality the critics are wont to ascribe to the term.
3. William Ralph Inge, *Christian Mysticism* (New York: Scribner's, 1933), p. 43.
4. As in Bruce Barton, *The Man Nobody Knows* (Indianapolis: Bobbs-Merrill, 1925).
5. Visions and voices are by no means a distinctive mark of mystical experience, although they are often connected with it.
6. Evelyn Underhill, *The Mystic Way: A Psychological Study in Christian Origins* (London and Toronto: J. M. Dent and Sons, 1913), pp. 157-92.
7. Pierce Johnson, *Dying into Life* (Nashville: Abingdon Press, 1972) gives an admirable and extensive interpretation of this concept in connection with various historic life styles.
8. Albert Schweitzer, *The Mysticism of Paul the Apostle* (London: A. & C. Black, 1931, 1953), pp. 10-13.
9. Inge, *Christian Mysticism,* p. 44.

## III. Philosophical Grounds of Mysticism

1. William James, *The Principles of Psychology* I, 221.
2. From the Korean Creed of The United Methodist Church.
3. W. T. Stace, *Mysticism and Philosophy* (Philadelphia: Lippincott, 1960), p. 68.
4. Stace, *Mysticism and Philosophy,* p. 34.
5. William Wordsworth, from "Lines Composed a Few Miles Above Tintern Abbey."
6. Quoted by Walter T. Stace in *The Teachings of the Mystics* (New York: Mentor Books, 1960), p. 20.
7. John A. T. Robinson, *Exploration into God,* pp. 86, 89-96.
8. *The Republic,* Book VII, 514-17.
9. *The Symposium,* 211. The translation is a paraphrase of the Jowett translation made by Charles Carroll Albertson and included in *Lyra Mystica:* An Anthology of Mystical Verse, edited by him (New York: Macmillan, 1932). There it appears in verse form, p. 7.
10. F. C. Happold, *Mysticism: A Study and an Anthology* (Baltimore: Penguin Books, 1963), p. 182.

11. *Enneade,* III, 8.9.
12. *Ibid.* VI, 9.5: 8.13; V, 5.12.
13. *Ibid.,* V, 3.14.
14. *Ibid.,* VI, 9.10.
15. *Ibid.,* VI, 9.11.
16. From the compilation by F. C. Happold in *Mysticism,* p. 196. He states that the translation is that published by the Shrine of Wisdom, Brook, Godalming.
17. *Ibid.,* p. 195.
18. *Ibid.,* p. 191.
19. Inge, *Christian Mysticism,* pp. 114-15.
20. *Autobiography,* XXVIII, 19.
21. Underhill, *Mysticism,* pp. 359-68.

## IV. Early and Medieval Mysticism

1. Willard L. Sperry, *Strangers and Pilgrims* (Boston: Little, Brown, 1939), p. xii.
2. Butler, *Western Mysticism,* p. 20.
3. *Confessions,* Book IV, viii, 13. Translation by E. B. Pusey, in Everyman's Library (London: J. M. Dent & Sons; New York E. P. Dutton & Co., 1907, 1939). Roman numerals indicate sections, Arabic the paragraphs, from the beginning of each book. Biblical citations are in italics.
4. *Ibid.,* Book VIII, xii, 28, 29.
5. *Ibid.,* xii, 30.
6. *Ibid.,* Book I, i, 1.
7. *Ibid.,* Book VII, ix, 14.
8. *Ibid.,* ix, 15.
9. *Ibid.,* Book VII, x, 16.
10. *Ibid.,* Book VII, xvii, 23. Here I have used the translation in Butler, *Western Mysticism,* p. 31 as transmitting the meaning more clearly than that of Pusey.
11. *Ibid.,* Book VII, xi, 17.
12. *Concerning the Nature of the Good,* Chap. 19.
13. *Confessions,* Book IX, x, 24.
14. *Ibid.,* x, 25.
15. *Symposium,* 211. See note 9 on chapter 3.
16. *Confessions,* Book X, vi, 8.
17. *Ibid.,* Book I, iv, 4.
18. *Ibid.,* Book X, xxvii, 38.
19. *Opera,* 1. John Herman Randall in *The Making of the Modern Mind* (Boston: Houghton Mifflin, 1926), p. 70 cites this injunction with its vivid language.
20. *The Song of Songs,* lxi, 2. Quoted in Butler, *Western Mysticism,* p. 97.
21. *Ibid.,* lxxiv, 5. I have used the translation in *Saint Bernard on the Song of Songs,* translated and edited anonymously (London: A. R. Mowbray & Co., 1952), p. 229.
22. *Ibid.,* lxxiv, 6, p. 230.
23. *On the Love of God,* Ch. X, "Of the Fourth Degree of Love." Translation by Terence L. Connolly in Kepler, *The Fellowship of the Saints,* p. 122.
24. *Ibid.,* pp. 122-23.

25. Quoted from Thomas of Celano, *Second Life,* Chap. vi by Underhill in *Mysticism,* p. 181. This author wrote two lives of St. Francis, the first in 1228 and the second some sixteen years later.
26. *The Little Flowers of St. Francis,* edited with introduction by T. Okey, Everyman's Library, pp. xi-xii.
27. *Ibid.,* p. xi.
28. *Ibid.,* Chap. xvi. Everyman's Library, pp. 29-30.

## V. The Fertile Fourteenth Century

1. *Treatise on Distinctions.* Translation by C. de B. Evans in *The Works of Meister Eckhart* (London: John M. Watkins, 1924). Subsequent quotations are also from the Evans translation unless otherwise stated.
2. Sermon III.
3. Tractate on *The Kingdom of God,* quoted in Rufus M. Jones, *Some Exponents of Mystical Religion* (New York: Abingdon Press, 1930), pp. 94-95.
4. In sequence these quotations are from Sermons IV, LXIX, LXXI.
5. From Sister Katrei, Sermon LXXXIII, and again Sister Katrei. This is a message of counsel and affirmation to a "daughter-in-the-Lord," about whom no further knowledge is available.
6. Quoted by Inge in *Christian Mysticism,* p. 156-57.
7. Sermon XXIII.
8. Sermon XVII.
9. Sermon XXVII.
10. Sermon I, as quoted by Underhill in *Mysticism,* p. 122.
11. *Ibid.*
12. Sermon IV.
13. *Works,* II, 160.
14. Quoted by Jones in *Some Exponents of Mystical Religion,* pp. 105, 118.
15. Sermons LXXIII, LXIX, LXIX, CIV, XLII, XI, XL, XII.
16. Underhill, *Mysticism,* p. 463.
17. Rufus M. Jones, *The Flowering of Mysticism* (New York: Macmillan, 1939), p. 102.
18. Tauler, Second Sermon for Easter Day. Quoted by Underhill, *Mysticism* pp. 217-18. By far the best recent treatment of the theme of dying into life is by Pierce Johnson in *Dying into Life: A Study in Christian Life Styles.*
19. Sermon for the Fourth Sunday in Lent. Underhill, *Mysticism,* p. 396.
20. Second Sermon for the Twelfth Sunday after Trinity. Jones, *The Flowering of Mysticism,* p. 102.
21. Sermon on the Feast of St. Matthew. In *The Flowering of Mysticism,* p. 96.
22. Sermon for the Fourth Sunday after Trinity. In *The Flowering of Mysticism,* p. 101.
23. Stace, *Mysticism and Philosophy,* p. 68.
24. *Theologia Germanica,* Chapter XLIV. Translation by Susanna Winkworth, found in numerous editions.
25. Chapter XLIII.
26. Chapter XV.
27. Chapter III.
28. Chapter XXXIV.

29. Chapter XI.
30. Chapter XXIV.
31. Chapter XIV.
32. Chapter X.
33. Chapter XLI.
34. Chapter XXXI.
35. Underhill, *Mysticism,* p. 465.
36. *The Book of Supreme Truth,* Chapter VIII.
37. Jones, *The Flowering of Mysticism,* p. 234.
38. *Ibid.,* p. 237, quoting from Thomas à Kempis' *Life of Gerard the Great.*
39. Book II, Chapter VIII. Note also the beautiful tribute to love in Book III, Chapter VI.

## VI. Protestant Piety Emerges

1. John Baillie, *A Diary of Private Prayer* (London: Oxford University Press, 1936; New York: Scribner's, 1940).
2. *Supra,* p. 113.
3. Pp. 258-64.
4. I have in my library *Devotions and Prayers of John Calvin,* compiled by Charles E. Edwards (Grand Rapids: Baker Book House, 1954). The selections are excerpts from Calvin's lectures on the Scriptures with accompanying prayers, but I fail to find in them what I regard as a mystical note.
5. See Pierce Johnson, *Dying into Life,* p. 73. His chapter on John of the Cross, entitled "The Inwardness of the Mystic," is a very illuminating interpretation.
6. So common is this experience in contemporary life that I borrowed John's title for a book of my own on this theme (New York and Nashville: Abingdon-Cokesbury, 1945; reprint in paperback, 1968).
7. Hence the relevance of Johnson's title, *Dying into Life.*
8. Quoted by W. R. Inge in *Christian Mysticism,* pp. 280-81.
9. *Ibid.* p. 280.
10. Kepler, *The Fellowship of the Saints,* pp. 313-14.
11. *The Devotions of Bishop Andrewes,* translated from the Greek by Dean Stanhope (London: Society for Promoting Christian Knowledge, 1901), p. viii.
12. *The Private Devotions of Lancelot Andrewes,* (New York and Nashville: Abingdon-Cokesbury Press, 1950).
13. These are excerpts from pages 23, 25, 30, 32-33, 40-41, 42-43 in the Abingdon-Cokesbury edition of the Newman translation.
14. *The Journal of George Fox* (Everyman's Library Edition; London: J. M. Dent and Sons: New York: E. P. Dutton, ), p. 8.
15. *Ibid.,* p. 11.
16. *Ibid.,* p. 134.
17. *The Fellowship of the Saints,* p. 498.
18. Quoted by William Fairweather, *Among the Mystics* (Edinburgh: T. & T. Clark; 1936), pp. 113-14.
19. See William R. Cannon, *The Theology of John Wesley* (New York and Nashville: Abingdon-Cokesbury Press), pp. 54-56, 61, 148.

## VII. Some Twentieth-century Mystics

1. Frank C. Laubach, *The Silent Billion Speak* (New York: Friendship Press, 1943).
2. Quoted in a pamphlet entitled "Meet the Apostle to the Illiterates," issued by World Literacy, Inc. Undated.
3. Frank C. Laubach, *Letters by a Modern Mystic*. Foreword by Alden H. Clark (New York: Student Volunteer Movement, 1937).
4. *Ibid.*, p. 11.
5. *Ibid.*, p. 14.
6. *Ibid.*, p. 24.
7. Laubach, *The Silent Billion Speak*, p. 1.
8. Biographical sketch by Lois J. Erickson in Toyohiko Kagawa, *Songs from the Slums* (Nashville: Cokesbury Press, 1935) Copyright renewal 1963 by Lois J. Erickson (Abingdon Press). Pp. 92-93.
9. *Songs from the Slums*, pp. 66-67.
10. *Ibid.*, pp. 89-90.
11. *Teilhard de Chardin Album*, designed and edited by Jeanne Mortier and Marie-Louise Aboux (New York: Harper, 1966), p. 8.
12. *The Phenomenon of Man* (London: Collins; New York, Harper, 1959). All data regarding his books are listed with the publisher and date of the English translation.
13. *The Future of Man* (London: Collins; New York: Harper, 1964).
14. *The Making of a Mind* (London: Collins; New York: Harper, 1965).
15. *Letters from a Traveller* (London: Collins; New York: Harper, 1962).
16. *The Divine Milieu* (London: Collins; New York: Harper, 1960).
17. *Hymn of the Universe* (London: Collins; New York: Harper, 1965).
18. *Teilhard de Chardin Album*, p. 77.
19. *The Divine Milieu*, pp. 73, 74n.
20. *Ibid.*, p. 95.
21. *Teilhard de Chardin Album*, p. 210.
22. Dag Hammarskjöld, *Markings* (New York: Knopf, 1964).
23. *Ibid.*, pp. 38, 49, 58.
24. *Ibid.*, p. 82.
25. *Ibid.*, p. 85.
26. For this and numerous other observations on Hammarskjöld's spiritual development I am indebted to Pierce Johnson's chapter entitled "The Dying Into Life of a Modern Man" in his book *Dying into Life*.
27. *Markings*, p. 205.
28. *Ibid.*, p. 89.
29. *Ibid.*, p. 90.
30. *Ibid.*, p. 205.
31. *Ibid.*, p. 13.
32. *Ibid.*, p. 100.

## VIII. Neo-Mysticism Today

1. Harvey Cox, *The Feast of Fools* (Cambridge: Harvard University Press, 1969), p. 104.
2. Hal Bridges, *American Mysticism: From William James to Zen* (New York: Harper, 1970), p. 151. Appendix A, statement by Swami Prabhavananda.

3. *Ibid.*, p. 15.
4. Quoted by Robert Campbell in "The Chemistry of Madness," *Life* magazine, November 26, 1971, pp. 67-68. Copyright: *Life* Magazine, © 1971 Time Inc.
5. *Ibid.*, p. 68.
6. Bridges, *American Mysticism*, p. 151.
7. William Kelley Wright, *A Student's Philosophy of Religion* (New York: Macmillan, 1935), p. 71.
8. Marcus Bach, *Strangers at the Door* (Nashville: Abingdon Press, 1971), p. 25.
9. Quoted by James Bissett Pratt in *The Religious Consciousness: A Psychological Study* (New York: Macmillan, 1921), p. 389n.
10. Emergent evolution also figures in the thought of Sri Aurobindo, another outstanding Indian scholar who did not visit America but spent fourteen years in England.
11. Bridges, *American Mysticism*, p. 76.
12. Daizetz Teitaro Suzuki, *Mysticism: Christian and Buddhist: The Eastern and Western Way* (London: Allen & Unwin, 1957).
13. Alan W. Watts, *The Spirit of Zen: A Way of Life, Work and Art in the Far East* (London: John Murray, 1936); *The Way of Zen* (New York: Mentor Books, 1959).
14. Daisetz Suzuki, *Essays in Zen Buddhism*, First Series (New York: Grove Press, 1961), p. 230.
15. See Philip Kapleau, *The Three Pillars of Zen: Teaching, Practice and Enlightenment* (New York: Harper, 1966).
16. Quoted in an article by Oliver Statler on "Pilgrims' Path in Buddhist Japan," in *Great Religions of the World* (National Geographic Society, 1971), p. 138.
17. Suzuki's elaboration of these characteristics of *satori* are cited in full in Stace: *The Teachings of the Mystics*, pp. 91-96 and in abbreviated form in Bridges, *American Mysticism*, pp. 103 f. The original with a fuller elaboration is found in Suzuki, *Essays in Zen Buddhism, Second Series* (Boston: Beacon Press, 1952), pp. 28-34.
18. The Soto sect of Zen holds that *satori* can be gradually attained, the Rinzai that it comes in a flash of insight. In the latter, students are sometimes jolted with sharp blows in order to help free the mind from other thoughts and become aware of their oneness with the universe.
19. Cox, *The Feast of Fools*, p. 104.
20. *Ibid.*, pp. 108-10.
21. "The New Rebel Cry: Jesus is Coming!" in *Time*, June 21, 1971, p. 59.
22. The extent to which this movement has made headway in the entertainment world is indicated by the fact that in one year Pat Boone baptized more than two hundred converts in his own swimming pool. *Ibid.*, p. 61.
23. Quoted by Martha A. Lane in "Jesus' People Speak Out," *Together*, December, 1971, p. 25.
24. *Glossolalia: Tongue Speaking in Biblical, Historical and Psychological Perspective*, by Frank Stagg, E. Glenn Hinson, and Wayne E. Oates (Nashville: Abingdon Press, 1967), pp. 78-83.
25. Marcus Bach, *The Inner Ecstasy* (Nashville: Abingdon Press, 1969).

# Index

## INDEX